... lecturer in film at the Polytechnic of Central London (PCL). His previous books include *A Long Look at Short Films*, 1967 (co-author with Derrick Knight), *WDR and the Arbeiterfilm: Fassbinder, Ziewer and Others*, 1981 (co-author with Richard Collins) and *British Cinema History*, 1983 (co-editor with James Curran).

Vincent Porter

On Cinema

Pluto Press
London and Sydney

First published in 1985 by Pluto Press Limited,
The Works, 105a Torriano Avenue, London NW5 2RX
and Pluto Press Australia Limited, PO Box 199, Leichhardt,
New South Wales 2040, Australia

7 6 5 4 3 2 1

89 88 87 86 85

Cover designed by Tony Benn

Phototypeset by AKM Associates (UK) Ltd.
Ajmal House, Hayes Road, Southall, London UB2 5NG
Printed in Great Britain

British Library Cataloguing in Publication Data
Porter, Vincent
   On cinema.
   1. Moving-picture industry — Political aspects
   — Great Britain
   I. Title
   384′.8′0941   PN1993.5.G7

ISBN 0 7453 0099 5

791.430942

Contents

For Lawrie and Alex
May the force be with you!

Acknowledgements

Many people have helped me in writing this book, some of them knowingly, many of them unwittingly. I owe a substantial debt of thanks to library staff everywhere, and in particular to those at the Polytechnic of Central London and the British Film Institute, who have always been helpful beyond the call of duty in searching out whatever books, periodicals or obscure pieces of information I needed. I also owe much to my students, who always expected complex ideas to be expressed simply and clearly. To my colleagues on the Cinematograph Films Council, who have argued with me over many policy issues and who will almost certainly not agree with everything I have to say, I also offer many thanks for making me look at some policy questions from a different perspective. Finally, I must thank my family who have borne without complaint the time I have spent at the typewriter and not with them.

Introduction

This book sets out to discuss how cinema functions in our society. It also describes the structures and organization of film production, especially those of Britain and the US. I have tried, as far as possible to present the arguments without using jargon or specialized terminology.

I begin with the various pleasures of going to the cinema, pleasures which are frequently taken for granted. I go on to look at the commercial and business factors which affect cinema ownership and the type of films shown, and follow with a description of the changing nature of cinema audiences, and what we know about the ways in which audiences respond to films. I then turn to the ways in which film production is organized, and the various struggles which have taken place over the last 80 years for creative control over film content. Against this background, the various measures which have been introduced to try and protect the British film industry from US competition are discussed, together with methods used by the authorities and the banks in their attempts to censor the content of the films we see. Then I turn to the ways in which the state has evolved particular forms of film patronage, both in Britain and elsewhere in Europe, and the ways in which film education has developed. Finally, I look at some proposals for change and argue for supporting those which are likely to promote cinema as a genuine cultural activity, both more pluralist in the forms and range of films which it produces and more accountable in the way in which it is organized.

I hope that this book will be of value to all those who enjoy going to the cinema and who also have a concern for the role that cinema plays in our society.

1. Pleasures

The cinema is magic. As we settle into our seats, the lights go down, the curtains open, the censor's certificate fades away and we are taken into a world where everything is possible. We open ourselves up to the pleasures of the silver screen. Image and sound, acting and spectacle, music and movement, fantasy and reality all combine to entertain us for an hour and a half or more. We can recall the images and the sounds in our minds long after the film has ended. A line of dialogue, an arresting gesture, the sweep of action or the melody of the soundtrack can all come flooding back to give us a small shiver of delight as we relive the experiences offered to us at the cinema.

One of the earliest tensions within the cinema was that between spectacle and reality, between fantasy and documentary. These twin possibilities have been with us since cinema began in the final years of the last century. They were differentiated most sharply in the films of the pioneering French film-makers, Georges Méliès and the brothers August and Louis Lumière. Georges Méliès was a puppeteer, a conjuror and illusionist; for him, the film camera was a machine for recording and creating bigger and better illusions than were possible on the stage. For the Lumière brothers, on the other hand, the film camera was a scientific toy which could record the comings and goings of the real world with an apparently objective eye. Workers leaving the Lumière factory, the Congress of Photographic Societies, a train entering a station – these were some of the subjects recorded by the Lumières. It was the latter example, a train approaching the camera placed at the edge of the platform, which left no doubt that the film camera was much more than a scientific toy. When audiences saw the film, they reacted as though the train would detach itself from the screen and enter the auditorium. The audience had, as it were, entered into the real world which the camera had recorded, forgetting that they were sitting in a cinema watching a series of images on a screen. Nowadays, of course, we are more sophisticated. We simply suspend our disbelief when the house lights go down and the film begins. One of the meanings implicit in the phrase 'it was a good film' is that during the whole of the film we were never allowed to remember that we were sitting in a cinema watching a film. We were simply absorbed in, and carried along by, the story.

The power of the cinema to take us into a world which we recognize as both realistic and credible, and yet bigger, better, more pleasurable, more terrifying or more chaotic than anything we have known ourselves, is both its great strength and its great danger. For cinema shows us simultaneously a world that was, a world that is and a world that might be. It is the past, the present and the future all rolled into one.

How can this be? Clearly the camera records an event (which film analysts call the pro-filmic event) which took place some time before we entered the cinema. The event itself may *appear* to be set in the past, or it may *appear* to be set in the future, as in a science fiction film. But whenever that event appears to be taking place, we know it actually took place long before we watched it on the screen. The conventions of film-making are such that great care is taken to eliminate from the image any evidence that it is artificially recorded. We cannot see beyond the studio set. There is no sign of the lights illuminating the scene, no sign of the microphone recording the sound, no sign of the several technicians involved in the production of the film. Great care is taken to ensure that there is a continuity between one image and another succeeding it. The actors' clothes must remain the same, the furniture and props used on the set must appear unchanged, and people must stand, or at least appear to stand in the same positions, relative to one another, as they did in the previous shot. Not only is the illusion of continuity between one shot and another carefully preserved, but also the film-maker will bind successive images into a unified narrative by dubbing a series of sound effects on to the recorded images. These may include an atmospheric background and a music track, all combining to weld the successive images into a powerful illusion of an imaginary world.

The soundtrack of a film does not simply serve to bind the

images of the film together. It is a source of pleasure in itself. The most obvious source of this pleasure is probably the theme music, and there is no clearer indication of this than the number of records and audio tapes of theme music sold. Many films are remembered for their musical themes rather than for the particular qualities of their images or of their stories. Classic examples are the zither theme played by Anton Karas to accompany *The Third Man* (Carol Reed, 1949), the music composed by Mikis Theodorakis for *Never on Sunday* (Jules Dassin, 1960) and the songs of Simon and Garfunkel for *The Graduate* (Mike Nichols, 1968). Hollywood has developed a whole genre, the musical, in which it is the songs and music played on the soundtrack which provide the primary inspiration for both creators and audience. A reciprocal cultural relationship has grown up between the film industry and the radio industry. The radio plays the music from the soundtrack of the film which simultaneously acts as a form of nostalgic reinforcement on those who have seen the film, and as a form of covert advertisement for those who have not. In some cases, the continuous playing and replaying of the music from a film on either the radio or stereo will cause even those who have already seen the film to go out and see it again and again. People have been to see films such as *The Sound of Music* (Robert Wise, 1965) as many as 25 times!

But films are more than simply sounds and images, they are movement too. Not for nothing does Hollywood call itself 'the movie business' or occasionally, when it is feeling pompous, 'the motion picture industry'. Movement in films comes to us in three different ways, which frequently overlap but which it is useful to distinguish. First, there is movement within the pro-filmic event. The action sequence involves either people or moving objects. People walking, running, swordfighting, boxing, wrestling, and riding on the one hand; car chases, aerial dogfights and spaceship attacks on the other. These are all part of the staple diet. Whole genres developed around individual skills such as the swashbuckler films which celebrated the art of swordfighting, or the western which grew out of a celebration of the skills of horseriding. More recently we have seen a new genre, the *Rocky* films, which are centred on boxing skills. Fight scenes are a key element in many films, and they are routinely not only a key element in the story, but are also carefully choreographed by the stunt men and women working on them. Similarly, car chases or aerial dogfights are carefully planned and executed with a view to maximum visual and aural impact. In the field of science fiction great care is taken with the special effects sequences to create maximum possible effect, for instance, of a simulated space attack. The *Star Wars* trilogy – *Star Wars* (1977), *The Empire Strikes Back* (1980) and *The Return of the Jedi* (1983) – is exemplary here.

A second means of expressing motion on the screen, is through the movement of the camera as it records the pro-filmic event. In the recording of a scene a camera can track from side to side, from a long shot to a medium shot, or from a medium shot to a close up, or it can track out. The development of the zoom lens has meant that by changing the focal length of the camera lens while filming, the camera can zero in on a small part of the image, or pull out from a detail to a long shot. Similarly, a camera can be placed on a crane so that it may rise up in the air to a high angle shot while filming, or alternately crane down from a high angle to eye level.

Over the years a complex set of modes of visual organization has been developed to transfer the dialogue in a film script on to the cinema screen. Individual directors have developed their own visual styles for expressing themes and ideas by means of the ways in which characters are placed in relation to one another or to the background, the ways in which the characters move within the image frame, and the ways in which the camera moves in relation to the action while it is recording the scene. These different planes of visual expression, the composition of the image, the movement within the frame, and the movement of the camera, offer the film director a complex means of choreographing the visual narration of the story. Visual style may be so distinctive that directors are recognized, and indeed celebrated, for their *mise-en-scène*, a term which was adopted in the late 1950s by the young French cinephiles writing for the magazines *Cahiers du Cinéma* and *Positif*, and which is approximately translated as 'putting on to the screen'. Despite working within the studio production lines of Hollywood, individual directors such as Vincente Minnelli, Nicholas Ray, Fritz Lang, Orson Welles and Otto Preminger all succeeded in giving their films a personal visual signature through the way in which they deployed these elements of the film-workers' craft to choreograph the narrative.

The third way in which movement can be created on the screen is by editing two shots together. The classical forms of film representation developed by Hollywood emphasize a continuity of movement and pattern as one shot gives way to another. A person or object which is moving on the screen is normally filmed from the same side in the following shot. The distance of the camera, or the angle of its point of view may change, but not the direction of the movement. Similarly, when filming two people talking together, the camera stays on the same side of an imaginary line joining the two people involved in the conversation.

The classical editing pattern did not develop by chance. It emerged as the dominant paradigm in Hollywood between 1909 and 1917 at precisely the period when the monopolistic Motion Picture Patents Company, which had formed a cartel of all the owners of the patent rights in film cameras and projectors, was being forced to give way to independent commercial companies who rejected the economic and creative conditions which the MPPC was attempting to impose on them. Film editing had existed before this period, but the emergence of the 'rules' – of not crossing the line of action; of changing the angle of the camera by about 30 degrees between one shot and another in order to effect a smooth transition; and of developing 'the eyeline match' whereby two people on the screen could be made to appear to be looking at one another by the choice of appropriate camera angles – were all developed in this period, especially between 1911 and 1913. Many of the independent film-makers were financed by cinema exhibitors, and it was a period when films developed from being technical novelties to become popular mass entertainment.

Other forms of editing were developed, however, particularly in revolutionary Russia where film-makers attempted to yoke revolutionary political struggles to revolutionary film forms. Particularly important in theoretical terms were Dziga Vertov and Sergei Eisenstein. The screening of Sergei Eisenstein's *Battleship Potemkin* in Berlin in 1926 brought a wave of critical admiration followed by a growing consensus among film critics of the 1930s and 1940s that editing was the basis of film art. The word 'editing' was not good enough for the film critics, however, and they introduced a new word, 'montage', into the English language to describe the technique used by Eisenstein. This worked on the principle of two shots *colliding* with one another rather than simply being *linked*, which was what his Russian contemporary Vsevolod Pudovkin, following the dominant Hollywood paradigm, had argued for.

The debates around the importance of editing in films sterilized western film criticism for years. What most critics had failed to notice was that however significant a film *Battleship Potemkin* may have seemed to them when it was first shown, the Russian people for whom it was made found it a bore. It was taken off four weeks after it opened in Moscow, and even when it was re-released after its spectacular critical success in Berlin, it only lasted for a further fortnight. The film that all of Moscow was watching in 1926 was United Artists' swashbuckler *Robin Hood*, starring Douglas Fairbanks, and made four years earlier by a virtually unknown film director, Allan Dwan.

It is now clear that most film audiences were looking for pleasures different to those of the majority of film critics. While most of us go to the cinema to escape into a world of fantasy and romance, or of action and adventure, the majority of film critics appear to look at a film as something to be savoured dispassionately, to be extolled for its formal beauties rather than to be celebrated for the sensual pleasures it offers. The editing practices developed by Hollywood, which work to hide the joins between successive shots and to involve the audience in the story of the film, make it an extremely powerful form of entertainment, both in the pleasures that it offers and in the opportunities it provides to manipulate the audience. 'The easiest way to inject a propaganda idea into most people's minds,' wrote Elmer Davis, Director of the USA's Office of War Information in 1943, 'is to let it go through the medium of an entertainment picture when they do not realize they are being propagandized'. One of the essential skills of a popular film-maker is to be able to strike a chord in our subconscious minds. A further requirement of the propagandist is to turn that bond which the film-maker makes with our subconscious into an action – possibly simply the refusal of an alternative action – which is deemed politically desirable. Propaganda can be devised not only to bring about change, but also to reinforce the ideological, moral or political status quo. And so film becomes the future, offering audiences models for their behaviour and world view.

One mechanism by which Hollywood sought to keep audiences coming to the cinema was through the film stars. The studios developed and marketed their stars to encourage audience loyalty to the output of the studio, who owned those stars by the virtue of exclusive and stringent contracts of employment. In the 1930s and 1940s one of the main ways in which audiences discriminated between the films which competed for the money in their pockets was according to the stars who played in them. Films were described as 'a Cary Grant picture' or 'a Bette Davis picture', as though the actual story of the film was of relatively little importance. Indeed, the story departments of the Hollywood studios made great efforts to ensure that the stories developed were suitable for the stars that the studios had under contract. In this way the persona of the star would accord with the role that he or she was playing, and the image of the star being marketed would be consistent over a period of years.

At the simplest level we may have an emotional affinity with the star which arises from the interaction of our own personality with the star and with the narrative of the film. When our involvement reaches the point at which we place ourselves in the position of the star, emotional affinity becomes a form of self-identification. This in turn can lead to the imitation of the hairstyle, the clothes, or on occasion the behaviour of the star, while in the most extreme cases, we become literally star-struck, trying to live our lives through our imaginary projections of the star's persona.

The film studios' need to create stars that were glamorous, desirable and identifiable has had a crucial effect on the social class of the roles played by film stars, for we tend to identify most strongly with the social class to which we aspire. We will identify with roles in our own social class when they offer us ways of behaving which we feel will lead to a happy and successful resolution of the problems facing us. Hardly ever will we identify with roles of a social class which we feel to be beneath us. Cutting across this class structure of our identification patterns, however, is a critical orthodoxy which celebrates 'realism', and in particular films which are deemed to be realistic in their representation of the condition of working-class people. Admiration for these films comes not from members of the working class themselves, but from liberal or left-wing critics who like to see their perceptions of the world portrayed on the screen. The films of the Italian neo-realists which emerged in the years immediately following the Second World War were a reaction against the studio-bound films of luxury and glamour. These were made while Mussolini was in power, by film-makers whose political persuasions ranged from communist (Luchino Visconti) to christian democrat (Roberto Rossellini). However, the films were mainly successful in London, Paris and New York, not in Rome or Milan. Italian audiences rejected the opportunity to identify with the tragic and miserable members of their own working class. Instead, they identified with Greta Garbo in MGM's glamorous anti-communist comedy *Ninotchka* (Ernst Lubitsch, 1939) which was supplied by the USA as part of its Overseas Information Programme. According to James Dunn, American ambassador to Italy, at the time the film was the most effective single thing in combatting the communist influence in Italy, thus helping to ensure that the communists were not elected to power in the country's first post-war elections in 1948.

The opportunity to identify vicariously with the trials, tribulations, adventures and exploits of the star is clearly one of the major pleasures of the cinema, and Hollywood has frequently used it for purposes which stretch beyond the bounds of the story itself. Our pleasure as an audience can, and often is, manipulated by the film-makers for particular ends.

Clearly one way in which film-makers attempt to manipulate us is to choose a story which represents wider political themes and values in a condensed form. Organizations like the USA's Office of War Information, and the United Kingdom's Ministry of Information, realized this and developed a covert strategy for propagandist films. They were following a tradition which Hollywood had developed a decade earlier. At Warner Brothers for instance, which had extremely close links with the American President Franklin D. Roosevelt, many films expressed in a coded and pleasurable way the politics of Roosevelt's Democratic Party and the philosophy of the 'New Deal'. The musical *Forty-Second Street* and the series of musicals that followed it, were hymns of praise to this philosophy, wrapped up in geometrically choreographed dance routines and perky, musical tunes. Later, as the US economy started to produce more goods, Warner's films became shop windows for the newest products of the automobile, domestic furnishing and garment industries, with tie-ins to encourage cinema audiences to buy the cars, the clothes, or the furnishings of characters in the story.

Frequently, however, Hollywood had to get its political and ideological messages across in more covert forms. One such period was during the late 1930s, when there was a conflict of commercial interests between Britain and the US in their struggle for world trade. When Germany started to grow and expand under Hitler, there were many in the US who felt that the best policy was to stay out of the growing economic, political and ultimately military conflict that was developing between Britain and Germany. The challenge for Warner Brothers, for instance, was to reflect the isolationist mood that dominated the minds of the American people and which was reflected in Roosevelt's political actions at that time, yet, at the same time, to make films which would be acceptable to the British public which constituted its largest overseas market. One way in which Warner's resolved this conflict was to mask the ideological messages of the films by setting them in key periods of Britain's past. The ambiguity of Warner Brothers' attitude towards Britain and its interests was reflected in a series of films starring Errol Flynn: In *Captain Blood* (Michael Curtiz, 1935) Flynn played a pacifist Irish doctor who suffered unjustly at the hands of English soldiers, the English Judge Jeffreys and was sold as a slave to an English plantation owner. In *The Charge of the Light Brigade* (Michael Curtiz, 1936) Flynn played a British army officer who tried unsuccessfully to alert his superiors to the dangers of incompetent British diplomacy and to slavish obedience in the face of stupid orders. In *The Dawn Patrol* (Edward Goulding, 1938), isolationist sentiment was expressed as a pacifist response to war, described as 'a great big stupid game that doesn't make any sense at all'. But it was perhaps in *The Private Lives of Elizabeth and Essex* (Michael Curtiz, 1939) that Warner's isolationist sentiments were most clearly expressed. The film was an extended debate between Queen Elizabeth I (played by Bette Davis, who advocated that England mind her own business), and Lord Essex (Flynn), who advocated intervention by the English fleet against Spain. To those who could decode the film, this was a moral parable about the tensions in Britain between those who wanted to appease Nazi Germany and those who wanted to fight fascism. By the end of the film, Essex has been condemned to be executed, since his desire for intervention does not reflect the best interests of England, but only his own self-glorification. As he mounts the steps of the scaffold he realizes the error of his ways. The film was released a month after Britain and France declared war on Germany. In his presidential campaign the following year, Roosevelt declared that the US was not going to become involved in any foreign wars.

By the end of the year, however, the situation was changing. London was being blitzed by Nazi bombers and Roosevelt was back in office. In Flynn's next film for Warners, *The Sea Hawk* (Michael Curtiz, 1940) there was an abrupt ideological reversal. In this film, Flynn became a dashing adventurer who tried to persuade Queen Elizabeth, played this time by the British actress Flora Robson, of the dangers of Spanish aggression. The ideological turnaround had been accomplished with finesse.

During the Second World War political allegiances changed beyond recognition. The USSR became the ally of Britain and the US in their struggle against fascism. Hollywood films such as Warner Brothers' *Mission to Moscow* (Michael Curtiz, 1943) and Samuel Goldwyn's *The North Star* (Lewis Milestone, 1943) portrayed America's new ally sympathetically. At the end of the war, however, came the Cold War. Partly as a result of the change in policy of the US government, and partly as a result of the investigations of the House Committee on Un-American Activities, Hollywood switched to turning out anti-communist movies. Over the next 14 years, Hollywood turned out well over a hundred of these. In 1952, at the height of the Korean war, it made over 20. Communists were routinely evoked as the enemy in thrillers, and these films unquestioningly reinforced these stereotyped images of evil.

One wonders how seriously this was taken by the average cinema-goer. Frequently, a film could simply change the labels without altering the basic structure of the story. One infamous case was *The North Star*, scripted by Lillian Hellman. It told the story of a collectively organized Russian village on the Polish border which came under Nazi attack. In 1958, the film was shortened, re-edited and re-released under the title *Armoured Attack*. But now it was an anti-communist film. The new producers deleted all references to Russia, and new material was added to Anne Baxter's final speech, in which she prophesied the coming of a free world for all people. The new footage included newsreel material of the Soviet army in Hungary in 1956 and a voice-over commentary stating that the communists were carrying on the traditions of the Nazis.

Film stories are frequently more complex than propagandists allow, however, and audiences are often able to take from the story those pleasures that suit them, ignoring those that do not. Some apparently non-political films are read as potent critiques of capitalism and its urban culture. One such genre is the private eye film which draws on the novels of Dashiell Hammett and Raymond Chandler, portraying big city life as corrupt, greedy, dishonest and immoral. In these films the private eye, driven only by a dedication to honesty, his own integrity, and the need to get to the bottom of the mystery, acts as and for the conscience of the audience. In his search, he exposes the evil and corruption that permeates big business, city politics and frequently even the police force and the judiciary. The star system and the narrative structure of the story work hand in hand to portray the seedy, down-at-heel figure of the private eye as a charismatic hero who is prepared to take any number of physical knocks in his search for the truth. What is more, his very poverty, his stoicism and his hard-boiled attitude in the face of big city corruption, combined with a spiritual purity, and above all a romantic idealism, make him a potent figure for identification by many members of the audience.

The pleasure of a satisfying story is perhaps the deepest pleasure offered by the cinema. Not only are we taken into the narrative where we can identify with the star, but the very story itself, if well told, can seem to offer solutions to some of our deepest concerns, thus recharging our emotional batteries. Narrative has been analysed in various ways. The Russian formalist literary critic, Vladimir Propp, for example, analysed a large number of Russian folk tales and concluded that in nearly all cases, the structure of the plots was similar. At both the beginning and the end of the narrative there were states of equilibrium; the narrative consisted of the progress from one state of equilibrium to the other. The change was brought about either by an event or by an 'enigma' that set the narrative in motion, and there were a limited number of ways of getting from the beginning to the end of the plot. Looking at the narrative from another perspective, the French anthropologist, Claude Lévi-Strauss, emphasized the way in which different anthropological elements are combined and resolved within the narrative. Oppositions such as male/female, good/evil, law/anarchy, individual/collective, wealth/poverty, happiness/sadness, and so on, are balanced against one another in myths and folk tales, forming a balanced and structured resolution of elements which frequently appear contradictory in real life. The narratives which endure are those that articulate a combination of elements which please the audiences or readers in that they apparently resolve personal and social needs.

Such mythical structures are mirrored in the major genres developed for the cinema. They may not be realistic, they may change and vary slightly from film to film, but it is the combination of cultural elements which seems to make them permanent and enduring: the adventure film offers us the possibility of victory over death and the unknown; the romantic film offers us the possibility of a world that operates according to the rules of our deepest desires; and the science fiction film offers us the possibility that we can shape and relate to the unknown.

The pleasures of the cinema, then, are many and various. Sights, sounds and movement are all welded together by the film-maker to excite and disturb, to thrill and to chill, to amaze and to reveal. Our attitudes towards film stars and the characters they portray are important in determining the meaning which we draw from the film, which in turn influences our view of the real world. It is not only government propaganda machines which have been ready to exploit the powers of the cinema for political purposes. Very often the film companies which finance and produce cinema films have made films with an eye to propaganda as well as profit. In the cinema pleasures and politics can be almost inextricably interwoven. For this reason, if for no other, we must take our pleasures seriously.

2. Screens

Cinema is a business in which the magic comes in exchange for our admission fee, and our pleasures are limited and selected for us. More prosaically, however, the magic may be a little tawdry. We may have had to queue to get into the cinema, or worse still not got a seat at all. If we tried to book in advance, we may well have been told that we couldn't do so, or that this would only be possible if we bought the most expensive seats. Once inside, we may have found that the seats needed to be upholstered, the screen was dirty, or sound was coming through the walls from another auditorium in the same complex. The floor might be littered with empty ice cream cartons or cigarette packets, or our enjoyment of the film spoilt by the rustle of sweet papers or crisp packets.

The cinema industry is in decline and has lost its confidence in the face of falling audiences. People now stay at home to watch television rather than go out to the cinema. Cinema staff are poorly paid, and it would be true to say that in many cinemas it is only the sale of sweets, cigarettes and soft drinks that turn a loss-making concern into one that is marginally profitable.

It was not always so. In the 1930s and the 1940s most people went to the cinema about once a week, and frequently more often. The coming of television and, more recently, the video-cassette recorder has meant that we now go to the cinema less and less. The annual cinema attendance in the UK is just over 60 million, less than 4 per cent of the figure it reached at the end of the Second World War. Families today spend about one-tenth as much of their household budgets on going to the cinema as they used to do 30 years ago. In contrast, the proportion of their money that they spend on electronic goods has more than doubled, while money spent on going to the theatre and to sporting events has remained approximately the same.

Not surprisingly, a large number of cinemas have closed. At the end of the war there were about 4,700 cinema screens in Britain; today there are less than one-third of that number. Cinemas are smaller than they used to be, and many are part of a multi-screen complex. Today there are on average about 400 seats in a cinema, whereas 30 years ago the average number of seats was about 900. In those days there was only one screen in each cinema; today two-thirds of all screens are in multi-screen complexes. Overall, there are just over 700 cinema sites in the whole of Britain, mostly in the city centres or large towns. The majority of local neighbourhood cinemas were closed in the 1950s. For many of us, a visit to the cinema involves an expensive evening out with a special trip into the big city. It is expensive to get in too – on average the price of a cinema seat has risen nearly three times as fast as the cost of living since the mid-1950s.

The population is rapidly being divided into those of us with access to a cinema and those without. Nearly 35 per cent of cinema screens are situated in south-east England while there are less than 9 per cent, in the whole of Scotland and a mere 6 per cent in Wales. Not surprisingly therefore, almost 50 per cent of British box office takings come from south-east England, with nearly 40 per cent coming from the London area alone. Here seat prices are higher too. On average it costs over twice as much to see a film in the West End as it costs in Wales and almost twice as much as it costs in Scotland. The declining number of cinemas means that cinema ownership in Britain is now concentrated in fewer hands. The main cinema owners are EMI Cinemas Ltd, which owns the 'ABC' chain of cinemas, and Rank Leisure Ltd, which owns the 'Odeon' chain. In 1982 EMI owned 119 cinemas (308 screens) and Rank 89 cinemas (225 screens); between them they controlled some 60 per cent of the cinema market. The remaining 40 per cent was dominated by Cannon Classic Cinemas Ltd with 61 cinemas (129 screens) and the Star Group of Companies Ltd which runs the 'Cinecenta' or 'Studio' cinemas and which has 49 cinemas (126 screens).

This concentration of cinema ownership is influential in determining the films we see. Each of the two major cinema circuits is 'aligned' to a number of film distributors who are able to offer them a regular supply of films. The circuits then have a continuous supply of films for their cinemas throughout the whole of the year. The EMI circuit is linked through Columbia-EMI-Warner (CEW) to EMI and Warner Films; through United International Pictures (UIP) it is linked to MGM, Paramount and Universal films. It also shows films released by the British company ITC. The Rank circuit is linked through CEW to Columbia films, through UIP to United Artists films, and through UK Film Distributors to Disney and Twentieth Century Fox films. It also shows any films released by its sister company, Rank Film Distributors. In 1983 the Monopolies and Mergers Commission found that this was a complex monopoly situation which operated against the public interest, but the government shows no interest in making any changes.

The monopoly relationship between the major circuits and the major distributors is designed to minimize the risks involved in releasing a new film. That is to say, it is designed to provide access only to those films released through this system. There is some limited evidence that this may be the reason why many people stay away from the cinema. In a survey carried out by the National Consumer Council in 1979, 28 per cent of of people questioned who said that they never went to the cinema claimed they would go to the cinema more often if there was a wider choice of films or a more frequent change of programme at their local cinema.

The public's choice of films in general is limited by the alignments of the cinema circuits and the major film distributors. In some places the situation is even worse. In towns and cities where there is only one cinema, this cinema effectively acts as the sole arbiter of the films shown. EMI controls 117 cinemas in these solo situations. Theoretically at least, the solo cinema owner can screen films from distributors aligned to either EMI or Rank, but in practice the choice may be further restricted by the availability of an additional print of the film to show in that cinema, or by the laziness of the booking manager.

The power of the two major circuits to control the films which are available to the public extends beyond their own cinemas. Before a film is released, the distributor and the cinema circuit discuss how it is to be released, what marketing strategy will be used and, crucially, in which cinemas the film may be seen. At this stage it is decided how many prints of the film are to be made, at which cinemas they will be shown, and in what order. If an independent cinema is in competition with one of the cinemas owned by the two major circuits, it will not normally be able to get a print of the film which is being screened by its circuit competitor until well after the public's demand has been exploited by the circuit cinema. This is often a period of five weeks or more. The independent cinema can, however, show films normally released on the other circuit, provided it is not in competition with one of their cinemas. If in one city there is an EMI but no Rank cinema, then the independent cinema may be allowed to show films which are normally released on the Rank circuit, but not those normally intended for the EMI circuit.

Independent cinemas may be denied access to a film for one of two reasons. They may either be 'barred' by a cinema from the major circuits, or the distributor may not have a print of the film available. Whatever the reason the net result is the same. When one cinema 'bars' another, this is written into the rental agreement which is signed between the cinema and the film distributor. As a result of the investigation of the Monopolies Commission in 1966, the film trade agreed not to operate a bar for more than four weeks, or for more than 16 weeks if it was a 'road show' film – that is, one filmed and released on the now rarely used 70 millimetre film stock. It was also agreed generally that bars should not extend beyond a 15-mile radius (25-miles for 70 millimetre films) unless they were registered with the Cinematograph Exhibitors Association (the trade association for cinema owners). Rank still maintain nine bars of over 15 miles radius. Six of these are in the West End of London. The other three are in Birmingham, Manchester and Glasgow.

Although it is the barring that attracts the attention of the government or the press most often, the availability of the film is likely to be a subtle but more substantial obstacle for the independent cinema owner. The print of a feature film can cost between £500 and £1,000, so the distributor will not make more than are necessary. It is often felt that the profits from a film are best made by keeping the film in one of the big circuit cinemas in a city centre for a long 'exclusive run' thus minimizing the number of prints that are struck.

According to a recent enquiry by the Monopolies and

Mergers Commission, only 50 prints were struck of *The French Lieutenant's Woman*. The film had exclusive runs for more than four weeks in ten provincial cities – and in one city it played for 22 weeks. In this case the film was denied to 58 independent cinema owners in the same cities. Even when a large number of prints are struck, as was the case with *For Your Eyes Only* (United Artists through Rank) for which 230 prints were struck, there were exclusive runs of more than four weeks in 13 cities, although in this case only 110 prints had been struck by the fifth week of the film's release.

Whatever the means, the truly independent cinemas are being squeezed out of the market by the duopoly which is operated by the two cinema circuits, and by the distributors who are aligned to them. Between them, EMI and Rank control 60 per cent of the British market, and the distributors aligned to them control an even larger proportion of film rentals. What independent cinemas want, however, is not just to broaden the choice of films available to the public, but to broaden the choice of venue for the most popular films. Fifteen per cent of interviewees in the survey carried out by the National Consumer Council in 1979 (those who also claimed that they never went to the cinema), said that they would go if the cinema was located nearer to their home. This figure was substantiated by a more recent survey.

The main additional outlet is the art house cinema. This normally shows foreign-language films which are subtitled rather than dubbed into English. Not surprisingly, the audiences are almost all middle class and well educated. In 1964, a survey carried out by *Sight and Sound* traced the exhibition patterns of three art house films – *Viridiana* (Luis Bunuel, 1961) *Last Year at Marienbad* (Alain Resnais, 1960) and *Vivre Sa Vie* (Jean-Luc Godard, 1962) – and found that there were 70 towns where one or other of them was shown. Art houses represented approximately one cinema in every 40. Soon, however, the British Film Institute started moves to build a series of local film theatres jointly financed with local authorities. In 1972 it was decided that these film centres should broaden their activity to include thematic programming, documentation, lectures and discussions and by 1976 there were 50 of these joint ventures. Some cinemas did not want to follow this path and left the venture at this point. There are currently 'public exhibition venues' in 30 towns jointly funded by the BFI and other local bodies, normally the Regional Arts Association or the local authority. Today an art house film can expect to play in cinemas in 42 towns; only 12 of these are not subsidized by the BFI.

In London there has been an expanding market for art house cinemas. The Screen group now has four cinemas; Artificial Eye has three. But the choice of films remains limited. Many of the London art houses are the venues where the art house distributors première their films. Those that are successful then play virtually all the art house cinemas round the country. In commercial terms however, almost 85 per cent of film rentals for art house films will come from London.

The London launch of an art house film is, of course, crucial to its success. To launch the film, a distributor will have to pay around £10,000 over and above any costs necessary for preparing a subtitled print and any advance guaranteed to the producer. Some art house distributors such as Artificial Eye pay large sums of money to secure what they judge to be the best European art house films, such as *Fitzcarraldo* (Werner Herzog, 1982), but increasingly they are also having to compete with television channels such as BBC2 and Channel 4. The producers of the most successful art house films are therefore looking to increased returns from the British market, either from the cinemas or from television, and they expect to be paid in advance.

Once the films have been launched, the response from the critics is crucial. Not surprisingly, a close relationship exists between the critics in the quality press and the art house distributors. The only mechanism for getting films into circulation outside the London hothouse is a grouping of 30 independent cinemas known as the Regional Consortium. The Consortium, which is independent but nevertheless serviced by the BFI, will liaise with small distributors in agreeing in advance to play a nominated film, in some cases advancing money to the distributor in order to pay for print costs. The risk to the distributor on marginal film titles is thus reduced and films which the public would not otherwise have a chance to see can be put into circulation. Films released, or re-released by this method include *Les Rendezvous d'Anna* (Chantal Ackerman, 1978), *L'Age d'Or* (Luis Bunuel, 1930) and *Fedora* (Billy Wilder, 1978).

Both in the popular cinema sector and in the art cinema sector, the market has declined in the face of competition from television. The shrinkage has meant that cinema-going has become more expensive and more heavily concentrated in London. Increasingly, the tastes of London cinema-goers have come to dictate the tastes of the rest of the country. Distributors have normally had the upper hand over exhibitors, although the increasingly heavy publicity costs necessary to launch a film in London's over-saturated entertainment market have meant that distributors too are having to make increasingly risky decisions. Only in the provinces it seems, where film-starved audiences are glad to be offered something different, can the BFI-subsidized regional cinemas hope to encourage the distribution of marginal films.

The standard accusation of cinema exhibitors and film distributors that television has taken the mass audience away from the cinema, was true in the past. Today however, television too has to compete with other types of entertainment for the public's attention. In a situation where all the different entertainment forms have to compete to gain our attention, the main winners are the advertisers.

3. Audiences

It is important to appreciate that over the years the nature and character of cinema audiences has changed. These changes in character are significant, for not only did yesterday's audiences consist of different individuals from those of today, but they came from different sections of society. When the cinema arrived in Great Britain, its initial appeal was to the working class. Cinema exhibition grew at the expense of the music hall and the cheaper type of theatre. In the big cities, particularly during the week, the audiences consisted largely of women and children. According to one estimate, about one-third of the children under the age of five went to the cinema once or twice a week. With the arrival of sound, the cinema moved upmarket. Capital was invested in building new cinemas in the middle-class suburbs rather than in the working-class districts, where they were designed to attract the more affluent sections of the community such as the growing number of office workers. The cinema became the staple entertainment of the average family and many families chose an evening out at the most comfortable cinema rather than choosing to go and see a particular film. This was the habit audience. Where they did choose to see a particular film, they made their choice according to the star of the film, from the trailer shown the week previously or because of the personal recommendation of friends. Less than one per cent knew the production company or the director of a film.

By the end of the 1930s men were going to the cinema more regularly than women. But although cinema-going was a regular habit, it was something that people could live without. A survey carried out in London, Reading, Brighton and Sutton at this time, showed that cinema-going was the activity that the lower middle class and the working class would be most likely to give up if money were short. By the late 1940s the profile of cinema audiences was changing once again. It was beginning to consist mainly of young people. But the advent of television, central heating and the mass ownership of the motor car meant that going to the cinema was ceasing to become a social habit. The cinemas that the big circuits chose to close were the local neighbourhood cinemas. The ones that remained open were those in the city centres. The staple audiences for cinema films became the young people who had money to spend but who couldn't afford a motor car and who wanted to get away from the family television set. By the early 1960s there were many more men than women in the audience. The proportion of those from the middle classes and those who had received some further or higher education was now substantially larger. Despite its popular origins, the cinema was becoming the entertainment for the young, the well-off and the well-educated.

The decline in cinema admissions also brought with it a change in the regional distribution of cinema attendance. Within the pattern of overall decline, the regions worst affected were Scotland and the north of England; the regions least affected were London and the south-east. As a result, an increasing percentage of the cinema audience was coming from these areas. Today almost half the cinema admissions in Great Britain are in this region of the country.

Today, of course, there are other places where we can see films. Nearly every home has a television set and an increasing number have a video recorder. In addition cable television and satellite television are becoming available. Although the upper and middle classes are well represented among the owners of VCRs, a recent survey by the Cinema and Video Research Consortium (CAVIAR) has shown that it is the lower middle and working classes who tend to use their VCRs more, and it seems that the people who watch the most films on video are young, male and less well-educated. The audiences who watch television vary, of course, from programme to programme, but in 1975, the BBC Audience Research Department estimated that the heavy television viewer was most likely to be female, working class and over 30; and many were likely to be unemployed.

Increasingly, people are taking advantage of the fact that they can see their films on different screens. Going to the cinema is only one way of watching a film. More precisely, going to the cinema is something more than watching a film – it has to be, since it is so expensive. In the 1984 CAVIAR survey, only 6 per cent of cinema visits were by people on their own. Back in 1975 the BBC survey found that only a quarter of those interviewed just liked going to the cinema. The others wanted an evening out with friends or relations, because they wanted to see the films that other people were talking about or because they couldn't see that type of film on television. Going to the cinema then, has ceased to be a habit. It is the young, the affluent and the better educated who go most often, and since it is expensive they look for a good evening out with friends, they choose the film they want to see. How then do they decide which film to watch? For most people, according to research by Thorn-EMI, the three main sources of information about cinema films appear to be the opinion of a friend or relative, a review of the film on television and the television commercial for the film. The most important of these is the recommendation of a friend or relative. This is not a new phenomenon. As far back as 1938, when going to the cinema was a habit rather than the special occasion that it has become today, people still sought the advice of their peers before spending the little money they had. 'In ordinary working-class districts', Herbert Morrison told the House of Commons, 'people look several times at 6d before they spend it at the pictures, and you find them asking people who come out at the end of the first house what the picture is like, and if the picture is bad, they do not go'.

A major study of women cinema-goers carried out in 1945 in the typical mid-western town of Decatur, Illinois showed that it was the 'opinion leaders' amongst their friends and relatives who were most influential when they chose which films they wanted to see. These 'opinion leaders' were three times as effective as newspaper reviews and advertisements and four times as effective as magazine reviews and advertisements in influencing their choice. In Decatur, the 'opinion leaders' were likely to be those women who went to the cinema most often and they were most likely to be moderately gregarious in nature.

Today, according to a recent study by Thorn-EMI, there is still no substitute for personal recommendation in getting people to go and see a film. The next most persuasive source, however, is a good review of the film, either on television or in a newspaper. For most of us, the film reviewer is someone whose opinion we feel we can trust. For the film industry, however, the reviewer is someone with whom they have to co-operate, but whom they would rather control. The more favourable the reviewer is to their films, the more likely they are to give the reviewer favoured treatment. This is not bribery, simply a way of ensuring that reviewers who are more favourably disposed to the type of films that they produce, get more facilities, more opportunities, more perks even, than those who are less favourably disposed. In 1946, George Orwell was of the opinion that, with one or two notable exceptions, the film critic was expected to sell his honour for a glass of inferior sherry. Today the price is somewhat higher; an indication, no doubt, that critics are slowly winning their struggles against the constraints the film trade seeks to impose. The relations between film distributors and the media are subtle and complex, and it is therefore sometimes necessary for a film reviewer to moderate his or her comments in order to survive. It is necessary for the critic to attend a preview of the film prior to its commercial release, so that the publication of the review will coincide with the public première of the film. Then, if the newspaper or magazine attracts the type of reader who might want to see their film, the film distributor will buy space in the magazine to advertise the film and thus help to finance the production of the newspaper or magazine. If the reviewer works for a television organization, it will probably be neccessary to show a short clip from the film in order to illustrate the review. These short clips are provided by the distributor free of charge, but it is the distributor who will decide which sequence in the film is to be shown, not the reviewer. Other facilities may be made available for selected reviewers. Interviews with stars or the director of the film may be laid on, and really favoured reviewers may be flown to exotic locations, all expenses paid, in order to conduct these interviews. How, with such lavish hospitality can a reviewer not be generous to the film concerned?

There are, of course, many reviewers who value their integrity and attempt to resist these gifts. But the film distributor has a range of penalties too which can be applied with discretion. It is not simply that the perks of exotic places and interviews with glamorous film stars can be withdrawn; in some cases film clips may not be 'available' for a hostile television reviewer. In extreme cases, the right to attend press interviews can be withdrawn.

In a *cause célèbre* of 1946, MGM refused to permit Ms E. Arnot Robertson, film critic for BBC radio, to come to any more of their press previews on the grounds that 'she was completely out of touch with the tastes and entertainment requirements of the picture-going millions who are also radio listeners, and her criticisms are on the whole unnecessarily harmful to the film industry.' Clearly MGM felt that Ms Robertson's reviews were damaging the commercial prospects of their films and they would therefore do all in their power to deny her any facilities to review them. The BBC, to its credit, stood up to MGM, and continued to employ her, but Ms Robertson sued MGM for libel and slander on the grounds that MGM had implied that she was an incompetent professional critic. She won her case in the lower court, but the decision was overturned in the Court of Appeal and the House of Lords.

A more salutary vengeance was wreaked on Graham Greene by Twentieth Century Fox and Shirley Temple for his review of their film *Wee Willie Winkie* (John Ford, 1937) which he had written for the magazine *Night and Day*. The film told of the conversion of an Afghan robber to the values of the British Raj by Wee Willie Winkie, a young girl played by Shirley Temple. In his review, Greene had pointed to the dubious coquetry of the way in which the role was played by Shirley Temple, giving a portrayal of childhood which was only skin deep and which knowingly masked adult emotions which carried sexual connotations for her admirers – middle-aged men and clergymen. Fox and Shirley Temple sued Graham Greene, the magazine and its printers for libel and they settled out of court for damages of £3,500 together with an apology. Greene's mistake, in retrospect, was to speculate on the feelings of Shirley Temple's admirers, rather than to concentrate exclusively on the merits or demerits of her portrayal.

The opinions of film critics and reviewers are therefore subtly constrained both by the laws of libel and by the commercial clout of the film distributors with the magazines or broadcasting organizations that employ them. Many of us are not consciously aware of these limitations, but if we don't have the opinion of a friend or a relative to guide us, it is to the critics and reviewers that we turn for advice.

Our third source of information is, of course, advertising. According to a recent survey, we nowadays turn most frequently to television commercials promoting the film. In a television commercial we have the opportunity to see pieces of action from the film, chosen for us by the distributor and the advertising agency. In the days when cinema-going was a habit, the film companies produced a trailer which was shown in the cinema the previous week. Today film distributors use television to advertise their films as well. This is a relatively recent phenomenon. For many years the film industry shunned television as a deadly rival which at best should be ignored, and at worst manipulated. Now, however, it has discovered that television advertising is one of the most effective ways to attract audiences. According to research recently carried out by Thorn-EMI, television is approximately three and a half times as effective as any other advertising medium for the cinema. Even so, the returns are not large. For every £1.00 spent on advertising, the distributor can only expect an increase of £1.90 in box office takings. However, in those television regions where there is more than 55 per cent of adults in the population, each £1.00 of advertising can bring in £2.75 at the box office. In other TV regions, the box office yield is a mere £1.20.

The relatively poor box office returns yielded by television advertising indicate not only our growing resistance to the claims of television commercials, but also the need for the film industry to compete with other leisure industries, such as pubs, clubs, restaurants, sports events – even television and radio themselves – for our attention. In terms of its total advertising expenditure, the film industry is fighting a losing battle. Its share of the UK leisure advertising budget fell from 20 per cent in 1978 to 13 per cent in 1982.

Even though we place advertising only third on the list of influences persuading us to see a film, our awareness that a film is being shown depends on the amount of time spent in promoting it. In the Thorn-EMI survey carried out in 1983, publicity budgets ranged from about £50,000 at the lower end of the scale for English-language art house films such as Breut

Walker's *Return of the Soldier* (Alan Bridges, 1982) or Merchant Ivory's *Heat and Dust* (James Ivory, 1982), to £600,000 at the upper end of the scale for a blockbuster.An advertising budget of £50,000 could expect to achieve an awareness of 10 per cent. Some films, however, did achieve a popular reputation which exceeded that which could be expected from their publicity budgets. Four films in this category were Varius AG/Sturla Leasing's *Who Dares Wins* (Ian Sharp, 1982), *Porky's* (Bob Clark, 1981), Paramount's *Airplane II – The Sequel* (Ken Finkelman, 1982) and United Artists' *Rocky III* (Sylvester Stallone, 1982). It may be significant that two of these were remakes of earlier successes.

The role of advertising in making us aware that a film is being shown influences our decision to see the film. The Thorn-EMI survey showed that for most films, a 10 per cent increase in awareness led to an extra £1 million at the box office. The major exception to this was Universal's *ET* (Steven Spielberg, 1982) which grossed a huge £20 million at the UK box office, and acquired a word-of-mouth reputation far in excess of that justified by its advertising budget. Clearly for some films, there is a breakpoint, a point at which we overcome our natural caution about spending money to see a film and decide that this is *the* film that we must go and see. We decide we will see the film, not because we feel we have made a rational choice, but because going to see the film is something that everyone around us seems to be doing. Our supposedly rational choice gives way to irrational imitation of those around us.

In general, however, our decision to see a film is a mixture of rational choice and media manipulation, orchestrated by the film distributor. Normally our rational choice takes precedence over the wiles of the advertiser. Nevertheless, some of us capitulate to what publicists call the bandwagon effect. If everybody else is going to see a certain film, then willy-nilly we must go too. We obviously look for a range of pleasures when we go to the cinema, but whether these are instantaneous and immediately forgotten, or whether they affect and influence the way in which we think and behave after we have left the cinema is a question to which we now turn.

4. Responses

The impact that a film has on its audiences has been, and continues to be, a matter for controversy both at a popular level and among experts. According to one school of opinion, films have a direct influence on their audiences, acting rather like a hypodermic needle to produce effects which can be anticipated in advance. This is the underlying philosophy of those who wish to censor the films that we see before they have an opportunity to 'corrupt' us. This is also the assumption of those who wish to use films for propaganda purposes, particularly in times of war or of political crisis. According to another school of opinion, however, audiences take from the films the pleasures, the emotions and the experiences that they need. This is the attitude of many libertarians who fear the political and social implications of film censorship, and of many producers, distributors and exhibitors, who fear the commercial implications of censorship decisions. Both sides are able to draw support from the experimental research which has been carried out so far.

Two major audience research surveys were carried out in the United States and came to opposite conclusions. In 1970 the United States Commission on Obscenity and Pornography concluded from the nine volumes of research which it sponsored that there was no correlation between exposure to erotic materials and established sexual attitudes or modes of behaviour, or between the availability of erotica and the incidence of sexual crime. Two years later, however, the Surgeon-General's Scientific Advisory Commitee on Television and Social Behaviour concluded from the 60 separate studies and reports which it had funded that there were indications that violence in programmes can lead to an increase in aggressive behaviour, but only in the short term and only under narrowly defined conditions which bear little relation to everyday viewing. Even this conclusion only emerged after what were reported to be tense and angry confrontations between the 'for' and 'against' factions among the experts. In the United Kingdom a review of the research evidence relating to screen violence which was published by the Home Office Research Unit in 1977 concluded that 'social research has not been able unambiguously to offer any firm assurance that the mass media in general, and films and television in particular, either exercise a socially harmful effect or that they do not'.

The relationship between films and their audiences is therefore a complex and subtle one and it has proved very difficult to design research experiments which are not open to serious methodological criticisms. Films are only one of a number of sources which can influence the ways in which we behave or which shape our attitudes and opinions, and it is extremely difficult for the researcher to design an experiment which can separate out the influence of a film from those of other mass media, of friends and colleagues, subsequent experience or even our own personal disposition. On the other hand, tightly controlled laboratory experiments in which the audiences are isolated from the influences of the everyday world are equally artificial, and therefore their results are equally problematic.

In 1982, however, one piece of research pointed to a correlation between the incidence of suicides by whites in the United States, and suicide stories in soap operas on US television. Similar correlations occurred between suicide stories in US television soap operas and both deaths and severe injuries in single-vehicle car crashes in the State of California during the three days after the programme was broadcast. This appeared to be clear evidence of a correlation between a particular event on television and the subsequent behaviour of some viewers. It is important to note that a substantial percentage of the people who watched the soap operas did *not* imitate the suicides shown in the soap operas. The precise psychological mechanisms involved in the imitative behaviour of those who did is still an open question. Did imitation involve a casual, indeed careless imitation of screen behaviour, or did the soap opera trigger a deeply felt and latent desire for suicide amongst those who were thinking of committing suicide anyway?

It is not difficult to find isolated instances where audiences have imitated behaviour which can be traced back to a recently seen film. A famous example was Universal's *The Doomsday Flight* (William Graham, 1966), in which a bomb was placed on an aeroplane by a man who then telephoned the airline and, in return for a large ransom, offered to say where the bomb was. The film was shown on American television in 1966 and on Australian television in 1971. After both screenings similar bomb threats were made in real life. There were extensive press reports of imitative behaviour of teenage violence after films such as Warner Brothers' *A Clockwork Orange* (Stanley Kubrick, 1971) and *The Warriors* (Walter Hill, 1979) and many other examples undoubtedly exist.

There are, nevertheless, two requirements which must be met before a person watching a film imitates the behaviour of someone acting on the screen. The first is that the person should know *how* to carry out the action that is being initiated; the second is that the person watching the film should have the *desire* to imitate the behaviour or action concerned. Looked at in this way, there are essential differences between the imitative behaviour of those who copied the events portrayed in *The Doomsday Flight* and those who copied the events portrayed in *A Clockwork Orange* and *The Warriors*. In the former, the film offered a means by which a person watching the film could make a large sum of money – a common desire in a capitalist society – without hurting anybody. In the latter two examples, the mode of violence shown was not particularly original, but the films did offer illustrations of teenage violence which may well have set off the violent behaviour of some teenagers who saw the films concerned. In all three examples, however, the impact of the films on those watching depended more on the values and assumptions which the audiences brought to the films concerned than on the actual portrayal of the events themselves. For the vast majority of the audiences who saw *The Doomsday Flight*, and who were essentially law-abiding, imitative behaviour was out of the question. For most non-teenagers and for many teenagers who were not violently disposed, the violent behaviour shown in *A Clockwork Orange* and *The Warriors* was something to be avoided or even deplored. In all the examples, the events portrayed were carried out by characters whose attitudes were opposed to those of conventional society; and in no case were the events imitated endorsed or condoned by the narrative of the film itself.

Films can influence audiences not simply by showing specific behaviour which they can imitate, but by offering attitudes and values of a more general and non-specific kind, which audiences may also seek to imitate. It is with regard to these less specific attitudinal changes that most controversy occurs as to whether films have any effect or not. In a well-made film, a number of elements may reinforce one another and thus convey a general message, attitude to life or behaviour model which are difficult for a researcher to untangle. The persona of the leading character in the film may be very similar to that of the star who is playing the role; the narrative structure of the film may well be centred around the actions of the leading character (film star) who, after mastering a series of obstacles and undergoing trials of strength, endurance, character or intelligence, achieves a happy ending by solving the crime, achieving his or her goal, capturing the boy/girl of his/her choice, or whatever. In much popular cinema, audiences look for films which package all these elements in ways which are realistic enough to be credible, but fantastic enough to be moving or exciting.

For most audiences the film star is a key element in this mixture. The intense emotional involvement with film stars experienced by audiences in the 1940s (as described in Chapter 1), has waned somewhat as cinema has taken its place alongside other mass media. But even so there are still strongly observable links between film stars and their fans which commercial interests seek to cement. Many film stars promote commercially branded goods, even though few fans today slavishly imitate the fashions, hair styles or make-up of their cinema idols. The same imitative syndrome has only been transferred to sports stars who can be seen on our television screens every week making the sale and manufacture of chic sportswear a multimillion dollar industry.

However, although there is clear evidence that many viewers, especially children, ape the clothes and mannerisms of film stars, it is by no means clear whether this imitation extends to other forms of behaviour. In two experiments using a B-movie – that is one without stars – carried out in 1957 and 1958, it was shown by observation of eye movements that the eyes of adolescent girls concentrated more on female figures and those of the boys on male figures. Afterwards, the boys remembered most about the aggressive and adventurous exploits of the male performers; for the girls, it was the romantic exploits of the females which they remembered best. This would seem to indicate that people draw from the films those elements which seem most relevant to their own situation and their own attitudes. But another experiment which set out to measure the relationship between the identification which audiences had with a particular film character and their propensity to imitate him or her, could find no correlation.

There is thus some evidence that people draw what they want from films, but reject that which they do not. Audiences seem to identify with those stars and roles with which they can empathize, but this term conflates the elements that are similar to their own personal situation and elements which are a projection of their own psychological needs. Audiences seem to be able to identify both with characters who are like themselves and also with characters whom they admire. The trick of the successful film-maker is to blend both elements into one character.

In films, then, there are characters which have attributes which are both reflections of the audiences as they are, and of the audiences as they would wish to be. For each individual member of the audience, however, the boundary between those elements which reflect his or her own reality and those elements which reflect his or her own wish-fulfilment will be different. The audience can be deliberately and carefully manipulated by building up tension or suspense and then releasing it, either by means of laughter or by cathartic violence. Film-makers such as Alfred Hitchcock built a career in mastering these techniques of audience manipulation.

A crucial element in this manipulation is the structure of the narrative, of the space it opens up between the central character or characters in the narrative, with whose emotional ups and downs the audience empathize, and 'other' characters and events in the narrative. Those 'other' characters and events which hinder or progress the main character and thus 'our' experiences and feelings, also carry with them other associations and connotations which may reflect attitudes about the real world of which we as members of an audience have no first-hand experience. They may be attitudes about politics, race, war, gender or sexuality of which we have little or no personal experience in real life, but which we unconsciously assume to be correct because of the role and position which they occupy in the narrative of the film. For instance, the enemy in many thrillers are 'communists' or 'Nazis' but the films tell us nothing about real communists – or real Nazis for that matter.

A number of research studies have shown changes in the attitudes and beliefs of film audiences after watching a film which led researchers to believe that films played an important role in changing audience attitudes. Research in the 1930s showed that the classic film *Birth of a Nation* (D.W. Griffith, 1914) induced adverse reactions to negroes, while First National's *Son of the Gods* (Frank Lloyd, 1930) produced a more favourable attitude towards the Chinese. Universal's *All Quiet On The Western Front* (Lewis Milestone, 1930) strengthened anti-war attitudes and in 1941, before the US had entered World War II, the attitude towards Great Britain of those who had seen MGM's pro-British propaganda film *Mrs Miniver* (William Wyler, 1941) was a massive 17 per cent more favourable than those who had not.

After the Second World War a number of propaganda films were made in Hollywood such as Twentieth Century Fox's *Gentleman's Agreement* (Elia Kazan, 1947) and RKO's *Crossfire* (Edward Dmytryk, 1947). The intention was that they should help to combat anti-Semitism and although studies showed that they did go some way towards achieving their aim, some read the films in the opposite way to which the film-makers intended. More recently, in a large study in North America involving more than 300 students, it was found that films had some influence in encouraging an acceptance of sexual violence. After seeing National General's *The Getaway* (Sam Peckinpah, 1972) and Medusa Cinematografica's *Swept Away* (Lina Wertmuller, 1975) the men, but not the women, were more likely to accept violence against women and to believe in the myth of rape – deep down women like to be raped.

In all of these areas we are dealing with attitudes that lie somewhere between the primitive and the civilized, between the irrational and the rational, between the unconscious and the conscious. Attitudes to people from different races and different cultures, to actual or potential enemies and, for men, to members of the opposite sex, all have a significant impact on the future of the tribe, of the culture, or of civilization as we know it. The changes in attitude which films can induce do not exist in a vacuum, however. They must compete with similar forces from other sources; from the press, from radio and television, from friends and from families. The changes in attitude which films bring about show a marked decrease over a period of time and a key factor in their effectiveness is whether they are reinforcing conventional attitudes and norms or whether they are setting out to change them.

The problem is that, for most of us, forces for attitudinal change usually operate at an irrational and unconscious level. This is particularly true where films are concerned. Most people do not go to the cinema to reflect rationally on the possibilities for changing their attitudes; they go to be entertained, to be occupied agreeably for two or three hours. Most Hollywood entertainment offers us a pleasurable story, in which the appearance of the real world, the horrors of the world as we fear it might be and the pleasures of the world as we would like it to be, are all subtly blended into a coherent narrative which, normally implicitly, but occasionally explicitly, assumes and endorses norms and attitudes which are frequently very difficult, if almost impossible, to disentangle from the story itself. The narrative structure of a film, its stars, its stunts and spectacles, the ways in which the characters are drawn, all shape and modify our attitudes. For what audiences do, when they see a film, is to apply a certain mental perspective to it, so that they can understand it – so that they can make sense of the world that they are offered. Most films work by reinforcing conventional assumptions. A few attempt to change the perceptions of the audience as the narrative develops. For a film to do this and to be popular is very difficult indeed. Another complicating factor is that many audiences are beginning to appreciate films in a more dispassionate manner.

Traditionally it has been either the subject of the film or its star that has encouraged us to go and see it. These assumptions date from the time when cinema-going was the principal form of mass entertainment. Since the Second World War, however, the cinema has had to yield this place to television. Its social role has changed and now it is the young, the affluent and the better-educated who go most often. This change in clientele is reflected not only in the type of cinemas and the choice of films that they offer, but also in the reasons for going to the cinema. Little research has been carried out in this area in Great Britain, but research in France has shown that the better-educated, and therefore frequently more affluent cinema-goer, is concerned to utilize his or her cultural capital when choosing a film. The most obvious way of doing so is to choose a film not for its content but for its author. Cinema ceases to be an entertainment or a piece of showmanship and is both categorized, and indeed valued, as a work of art. For most films the author is seen as being the film director. This is certainly true for foreign-language films and is reflected in common parlance. People talk about 'the new Godard' or 'the latest Bergman', while books about film directors and their films are to be found in most bookshops, even in cities where their films are never shown. But increasingly Hollywood films are also categorized by their director. Alfred Hitchcock, who was both a producer and a director, ensured that his name went above the title of the film; other Hollywood directors such as Sam Peckinpah, Martin Scorcese and Steven Spielberg are widely known.

In part, this awareness of film directors' names is a means of choosing films with a distinctive style, but it also permits and ensures comparisons between films made by the same director for similarities and differences in their visual style and in their recurrent use of underlying themes and motifs. These considerations which extend the appreciation of the subject of the film to its thematic and stylistic similarities with other films made by the same director, frequently draw on analytical methods developed for other art forms such as painting, literature or the theatre, which allow the better-educated to apply their cultural critera to the selection, appreciation and subsequent discussion of films.

In the days when cinema was a genuine popular art, before it gave way to television, connoisseurship of films existed at a popular and untheorized level. Hollywood for its own industrial reasons developed a number of genres which developed and reworked a number of standard subjects and themes. Audiences recognized, and appreciated the forms of repetition and differences between different films within the same genre. Westerns, musicals, gangster films, melodramas, comedies and thrillers were not only the standard fare for cinema-goers, but permitted the more perceptive observers to comment upon the similarities and differences within each genre. Frequently of course, this led the more percipient to realize that some of these differences were a reflection of the studio that produced the film, the scriptwriter who wrote it, or the director who shot it. These experts were only a very small minority, however, and it is significant that it was French film critics associated with the magazine *Cahiers du Cinéma* who first began to categorize Hollywood films by their director in the 1950s. Not only did they come from a culture which considered film to be an art, but for them, Hollywood films were part of a foreign culture – albeit a predatory one – from which they were able to distance themselves quite easily and thus make coherent analytical distinctions between films. Films came to be savoured reflectively rather than consumed avidly.

This reflective savouring of a film, comparing its qualities with others by the same director, or of the same period, or reflecting upon the way in which the story is expanded as a narrative, or is conveyed through the deployment of visual style, is, of course, vastly different from taking in a straightforward and naive pleasure in the story the film has to tell and the emotions it induces. It is an acquired skill and it is in the capital cities of the world, in London, New York, Paris and Berlin that these tastes are formed and consolidated. Certain directors and certain films become part of a canon of classical cinema that is shown and reshown in repertory cinemas, film societies and colleges, written about in books and magazines and discussed in television programmes.

A neat illustration of this process at work is illustrated by the two films *Psycho* and *Peeping Tom*. The former was made by Alfred Hitchcock for Paramount, the latter was made by a British director, Michael Powell, for his own production company. Both films were released in 1960 and both attracted the reproach of critics for their mixture of violence and sadism. In *Psycho* Marion Crane (Janet Leigh) steals some money and is stabbed to death while having a shower by Norman Bates (Anthony Perkins) who is later caught by the police, having gone completely mad. In *Peeping Tom*, Mark Lewis (Carl Boehm) who has had a psychologically disturbed upbringing enjoys filming pretty women and recording their deaths in close-up as he kills them with a knife-blade attatched to one of the tripod legs of the camera. *Psycho* was written about extensively, and the first English-language book on Hitchcock's films was published in 1965. *Peeping Tom* received a few laudatory reviews in minor critical magazines, while some of the more perceptive criticism is found in a book on British cinema published in 1970. A season of his films at the National Film Theatre followed. In 1978 a book was published on Michael Powell and his scriptwriter on several of his other films, Emeric Pressburger.

Both films were taken up by highly theoretical film journals as examples of films which explored the nature of film language and the voyeuristic nature of the relationship between the event filmed, the camera and the emotions of the spectator. Accordingly the two films are now regularly seen and screened for students on film courses and in many film societies.

In other parts of the film establishment, the film-makers were honoured for their contributions to cinema. Alfred Hitchcock received a knighthood, and in 1971 was made a Fellow of the British Academy of Film and Television Arts. Michael Powell and Emeric Pressburger were made Fellows of the British Academy of Film and Television Arts in 1981 and Fellows of the British Film Institute in 1983. The two films concerned, *Psycho* and *Peeping Tom* had not changed in any way. What had changed, and what continues to change is society's response to these films and to the cinema in general.

A separate but parallel response is the emergence of the cult film. This is normally a film which has been a disaster either with the critics or at the box office, or one which was produced as a low-budget exploitation movie. They are then taken up by minority audiences who will go and see them time and time again especially at late-night screenings. These audiences, often young and middle class, sometimes gay and sometimes straight, celebrate the trash aesthetics of the films, their ludicrous plots or their camp qualities. A good example is Twentieth Century Fox's *The Rocky Horror Picture Show* (Jim Sharman, 1975) which was adapted from the stage play of the same name by Richard O'Brien. The film has generated a faithful following and has developed a form of audience participation which involves dressing up as characters from the film, recreating the actions of the film in front of the screen, shouting particular lines that either anticipate or comment upon the action of the film and throwing rice or confetti at appropriate points within the film. A special record album of the film soundtrack together with a set of suggested responses has been issued and there is now a special subculture of fans of the film.

Initially, the audience for the film was the gay community in the US, but the film's cult status has now spread to Australia and South Africa, largely, it appears, through the merchandizing of the soundtrack album and references to the film in both the cinema film and the television spin-off series of MGM's *Fame* (Alan Parker, 1980). The cult has now reached the United Kingdom where it appears to attract a mainly white middle-class audience of both straights and gays, and where *The Rocky Horror* seems to offer audiences the opportunity to act out and perform fantasies. The film, which cost Fox approximately $1 million to produce, has made over $30 million in North America alone.

The cinema has ceased to be the medium of entertainment for the masses and now caters to all social classes as well as specialist minority groups. Our responses to films are also more complex. Although many films continue to have a strong influence on our behaviour and our attitudes, we now take a more relaxed view of film content. This is especially so if the film concerned can be recuperated as art rather than entertainment as the case histories of *Psycho* and *Peeping Tom* both show. The main concerns of the moralists and the politicians lie elsewhere, with television and with video cassettes; to some extent, these will determine social attitudes to cinema films as we shall see in a later chapter. None the less, it remains broadly true that an enthusiasm for the cinema is no longer seen as a sign of psychological dependence but, more often as a mark of culture and taste.

5. Production

When the technology of the film camera and the film projector was developed at the end of the nineteenth century, both of these technologies were protected by patents. Different elements in these technologies were developed in the US, France and Great Britain, and in the early years of cinema, commercial power within the industry depended on the sale of film cameras or film projectors. It took the industry several years to realize that there were commercial benefits to be obtained from standardizing the camera and projector technologies so that the films which were made to be shown on one firm's technology could also be shown on another. From that moment on, attention switched from the technology itself to the films.

Standardization of technology led first to a monopoly in the supply of the film stock on which the images were recorded and reproduced. The patent in the 35 millimetre sprocketed film stock was owned by George Eastman and it was on this patent that the fortune of the Eastman Kodak Picture Company was built. Over the years, Kodak built up a multi-national company specializing first in photographic stocks and equipment and later in other technologies. Kodak, like many American companies, was strongly anti-union in its attitudes, and nowhere did it prosecute these attitudes more openly than at its factory at Harrow on the north-west outskirts of London where it started making motion picture film in the late 1920s. When several of its workers joined the Association of Cinematograph Technicians (ACT, later ACTT when it began to organize television as well as film technicians in the mid-1950s) in search of better wages and working conditions after the Second World War, Kodak resisted strongly. Until that time its strategy towards the 5,000 workers employed in its Motion Picture Division had been one of benevolent paternalism. What the workers had been offered were privileges and benefits which were designed to encourage them to be loyal to Kodak's interests, but which, on the other hand, gave them no substantial rights. During the war a workers' production committee had been set up as part of the general war effort to improve productivity, and this, Kodak argued, was an adequate vehicle for industrial relations matters. Kodak required its workers to wear numbers on their hats while they were working in the processing plant in order to make sure they didn't steal each other's uniforms and it employed a system of giving each worker 'marks' for good behaviour.

In 1949, the film technicians trade union, ACT, set up a Kodak branch, and over the next 20 years Kodak seemed determined to impede trade unionism at its Harrow factory. Kodak involved themselves on one occasion in a curious saga. Ken Roberts was Chairman of ACTT's Kodak branch. He appears to have been someone who could not be simply sacked for bad behaviour. Despite his trade union activities and political beliefs, in all other ways he would have been regarded as a very good employee. On one occasion, he received £100 from Kodak who had taken up a suggestion he had made for improvements. In November 1964, however, Roberts and a fellow trade unionist employed by Kodak, Geoff (Godfrey) Conway, were arrested by police and later brought to trial on charges of conspiracy to contravene the provisions of the Prevention of Corruption Act and to injure Kodak Limited. A few days after the arrest they were summarily dismissed by Kodak. At the end of the trial at the Old Bailey some three months later, Ken Roberts and Geoff Conway, who had both been accused of passing Kodak industrial secrets to the agent of an East German firm, Diachemie, were unanimously acquitted by the jury of all charges brought against them.

Some extraordinary facts came out of the trial. Kodak themselves had agreed to pay the chief prosecution witness, a Belgian, M. Jean Paul Soupert, some £5,000 to come to Britain and give evidence for the Crown. The agreement provided that Kodak would consider a bonus payment 'depending on the assistance and satisfaction given by you in carrying out these arrangements'. It further emerged at the trial that the British security services, two of whose members had been assisted by Kodak's security adviser in their investigative work, had apparently, in liasion with Belgian security, arranged for false date stamps to be put in Soupert's passport to enable him to say he had been in London on two days when he had not been in Great Britain at all.

After the acquittal ACTT tried to get Ken Roberts and Geoff Conway reinstated but without success. It was not until December 1973, that ACTT managed to make Kodak sign a limited recognition agreement, following several months of industrial struggle in which the TUC gave its official backing, the print union SOGAT imposed restrictions on Kodak materials, the Television Branch of ACTT switched to non-Kodak newsreel stocks, the TGWU Dockers and Drivers section imposed severe blackings on both Kodak goods and supplies, and both SOGAT and NGA members made sure that Kodak's house journal was not printed. It had taken 30 years and the combined strength of the British trade union movement for ACTT to achieve even partial recognition by Kodak.

If George Eastman had built Kodak's fortune on his patent monopoly of sprocketed motion picture film, other magnates set out to build their empires, not on the celluloid base on which images were recorded and stored, but on the film images themselves. In order to do this, they too had to secure some form of legal protection for their images. The answer was the law of copyright. Copyright law had originally been designed to protect the creative work of authors, composers and artists. One of the technical advantages of George Eastman's photographic stock was that it could be copied and reproduced an almost indefinite number of times. But its technical advantages were a financial liability. Nobody would invest in film production unless their investment could be protected from being copied without their approval. It was necessary to protect film companies and their investors by extending the law of copyright to film since, as the Patents Committee of the United States Congress noted in 1912, 'the money invested (in film production) is so great and the property rights so valuable'. Accordingly, copyright protection was extended to the corporation making the film not only throughout the United States but, by means of the International Copyright Conventions, throughout nearly every country in the world.

By granting copyright protection to film, however, the US

legislature not only protected the interests of the bankers who wanted to invest in film production, it also confirmed the copyright interests of those employees who were making a creative contribution to the films on which they worked. Employees who had something to contribute other than their labour, were entittled to their own copyright. Chief among these contributors was the writer. Whether the film was made from a previously published novel or play, or from an original script, the producer had to buy the copyright in the original work. Given the large sums involved in production, however, the production companies began to negotiate exclusive rights, so that they alone had the film rights to a story. The more successful companies not only bought exclusive rights to all the stories they wanted to film, thus preventing any competition, but they also bought the film rights to many stories they did *not* want to film, to prevent their rivals from acquiring the rights. Many best-selling books and plays were never even turned into film scripts, let alone finished productions.

Copyright law was a form of legislation which the motion picture corporations were able to use to their advantage. More difficult was their need to build up a large scale organization capable of mass producing films which would regularly satisfy the markets of the world. They were able to raise loans both from the banks and from Wall Street by using the real estate value of their big city centre cinemas as security. This gave them enough finance to produce a regular supply of films both for their own cinemas, and for independent cinema owners who were only too glad to show their films either on a second- or third-run basis, or on a first-run basis in cities where the corporations had no cinemas of their own. But money was not enough. The creative skills and capabilities of their workers had to be organized so that the corporations could offer the market a regular supply of films which would all be profitable, and yet individually distinct. This meant the recognition of two very separate but interrelated factors. First, insofar as it was possible, they had to control the marketplace. Second, the creative skills of the work-force had to be controlled so that they produced the films that the marketplace seemed to want.

The marketplace in films is between film distributors – or renters – and cinemas. Films are not bought and sold as such.

Cinemas are licensed by the renter to show a film for a certain period. It may be a month, a week, or a few days. The major film renters built up their control of the market in a number of ways: by producing a large and regular supply of films; by insisting that cinemas show both the good and the bad films by introducing block and blind booking; by controlling the publicity advertising the films, including publicity about the film stars; and by demanding a larger rental from the cinemas for the more successful films, thus ensuring that cinemas could only retain modest profits. Cinemas, dependent on the renters for a regular supply of films, became the shop window for these films. Outside the US, the film distributors opened up their own subsidiaries so as to control the supply of their films to foreign cinemas. Conversely, European banks preferred to invest money in building cinemas rather than in film production; they could always rely on films which had proved a commercial success in the United States market.

By means of these strategies the major US distributors – MGM, Warner's, Twentieth Century Fox, Paramount, RKO, Universal and Columbia – were able to control first the US market and later much of the world market. In turn, they were able to feed all of their market intelligence back into designing and shaping the films that they wanted their production arm to make. In 1947, however, the US Supreme Court handed down an anti-trust ruling which separated production and distribution from exhibition. At the same time, cinema audiences began to fall off as audiences in the USA switched to television. The major US distributors retained their control of the marketplace by cutting back on production, thus keeping cinemas comparatively short of good films at a time of market decline, and by commissioning independent producers to make films for which they would put up part of the finance in return for the rights to distribute the film. They would also control all publicity and take on average a 30 per cent distribution commission over and above all expenses incurred. In this way independent producers were given a limited degree of creative control in return for a financially punitive distribution contract.

In the early days, however, the financial relations between the production and distribution arms of the US majors were simply a matter of internal bookkeeping. The profits of both the distributors and the producers ended up in the same pocket. I was the creative control over its product that concerned the movie majors. In order to gain this, it had to organize a large work-force on a production line basis, where many tasks required both artistic and craft skills. To this end they adopted a system of scientific management, or 'Taylorism' named after its founder Frederick Winslow Taylor.

The principles of scientific management were first applied to the production of films by Thomas Ince between 1911 and 1916 at the Hollywood studios of the New York Motion Picture Company. The key to scientific management was the shooting script for the film which became the 'blueprint' for production. The script was budgeted and its shooting scheduled for production. The director of the film was then issued with the shooting script which he was told to 'shoot as written'. The beauty of this method from the point of view of corporate management was that the control of a number of films could be maintained by the studio head, or a very few senior producers. The scripts were prepared by scriptwriters, according to the general guidelines laid down by the studio head, which he, in turn, related to the general needs of the market as relayed to him by the distribution department. Once finished, the script could be distributed to all the departments for pre-planning which could then prepare a budget, a shooting schedule and design the sets and the costumes. Once these were agreed, the sets could be built and the director allowed to supervise the actual shooting. During shooting the producer could maintain control by watching the 'rushes' or 'dailies' of each day's shooting, and ordering re-shoots if necessary. Only then could the old sets be struck and the new ones built in their place. Finally, the editor could supervise the assembly of the rushes, first into a rough cut then into a fine cut and finally into a fully dubbed version complete with sound effects and music.

At each stage the producer would approve the film or make changes as necessary. Sometimes the distribution department would suggest changes. In cases of doubt, a film would be given a sneak preview to members of the public, and according to its reception, might be shortened or lengthened, or certain sequences might be dropped or, on rare occasions, new material added.

This method of organizing production and the division of labour ensured that the producer was able to oversee all stages. The people making the film were divided into two categories – those who played a major part in shaping and creating the film, and those who only played a supporting role. In the former category were the producers, the stars, the writers, the directors and a few senior technicians. The latter category consisted of everyone else, from projectionists to plasterers, from cameramen to carpenters.

The initial philosophy of the major Hollywood corporations, like that of Kodak, was to prevent trade unionism which was inimical to their interests. They wanted to keep Los Angeles what they termed 'an open city', that is, one where labour was not allowed to organize into unions. Resisting this anti-union policy, the American Federation of Labour (AFL) set out to organize the studio construction grades and following a number of strikes, an agreement was negotiated in November 1926 between the major film studios and five unions: the International Alliance of Theatrical Stage Employees and Moving Picture Machine Operators (IATSE); the United Brotherhood of Carpenters and Joiners (UBCJ); the International Brotherhood of Electrical Workers (IBEW); the International Brotherhood of Painters and Paperhangers (IBPP); and the American Federation of Musicians (AFM). This agreement, commonly known as the Studio Basic Agreement formed the basis of industrial relations in Hollywood.

The agreement established a system whereby the presidents of the five unions who signed the agreement met with five employers' representatives who would then handle any labour relations problems including minor grievances, wages, hours of employment or working conditions. The snag in this arrangement from the point of view of the ordinary studio worker was that the agreement specifically forbade shop stewards or local business agents to handle any disputes directly. All disputes had to be handled centrally. The producers had insisted on this in order to avoid inter-union disputes, but the result was that many problems which arose on the studio floor failed to get resolved; either the president of the union declined to put them forward or the producers were unwilling to compromise. IATSE in particular was an extemely dictatorial organization and its president from 1934, George Browne, and his personal representative, a former Chicago gangster called Willie Bioff, were later jailed for extortion. Bioff, who was personally appointed by Browne, brought many of his old ways to Hollywood and it was later admitted at their trial that they had received bribes from a producer not to bring grievances by certain of their members up to the disputes committee.

It was not surprising in this climate that the dominance by IATSE of Hollywood's labour organizations was challenged by other groups, since the industrial power base of IATSE lay outside Hollywood itself through its organization of cinema projectionists. Following an inter-union dispute at Paramount over a cameraman who was asked to travel around the country taking shots of airports, IATSE called out its projectionists and closed down all of Paramount's cinemas. Paramount was forced to settle, but IATSE's price was high. It demanded and got a closed shop agreement for all its members. By 1936 IATSE's membership had increased to 12,000 and it was squeezing out the smaller craft unions affiliated to AFL.

In April 1937 the AFL-affiliated craft unions formed a loose alliance called the Federated Motion Picture Crafts (FMPC). It consisted of actors, painters, make-up artists, hair stylists, art directors, draughtsmen and labourers. Led by Herbert Sorrell, the FMPC called a strike some three weeks later, demanding recognition of their respective unions and a wage increase. IATSE moved to break the strike by recruiting striking members of the FMPC and put them into the same jobs as IATSE members at a higher wage. After six weeks the strike collapsed, although some groups had obtained recognition, but not as affiliates of the FMPC.

The significance of the inter-union disputes was that if the FMPC strike had succeeded, it would have led to a more localized form of union-management agreements, which could have given the craft workers some control over the conditions of their labour. The massive centralized system, favoured by the studio managements and by IATSE, enabled unions to negotiate for high wages for their members, but it gave individual technicians virtually no control over the conditions under which they had to work. The number of people working on a film, the pace at which the film had to be made, the equipment allocated for production, the length of the working day, the breaks allowed for meals or for sleep, were all beyond their control.

The struggle between the two factions and philosophies continued however. The FMPC was reformed as the United Studio Technicians Guild (USTG) and in 1939 the National Labor Relations Board held an election to decide whether they or IATSE should represent the 12,000 studio technicians. IATSE, still under the leadership of Browne and Bioff, won. Bioff accused the USTG of being a communist front organization, and when he left Hollywood in 1940 to serve his sentence he claimed that he had been 'framed' by communists and 'moneyed interests'.

The studio employers were heavily involved in the bribe scandals and the inter-union disputes. It was they who paid the bribes to Willie Bioff and encouraged the corrupt and dictatorial methods by which he and Browne ran IATSE. They later acknowledged that the bribes paid to Bioff, in return for which he held back applications for wage increases, and in some cases even authorized wage cuts, had saved the studios about $15 million. There is no doubt too, that they were also heavily implicated in Bioff's communist smear campaign against the USTG, a charge which was taken up after the Second World War against its successor, the Conference of Studio Unions (CSU), by the infamous House Committee for Un-American Activities.

The aims of the CSU were to unite the motion picture unions for the protection of the autonomy of each and to advance through joint consultation and action the economic welfare of the motion picture unions and their members. Its constitution provided that if any member union went out on strike, no member union of the CSU would cross picket lines. This gave many of the smaller unions the economic strength to bargain through collective support from other groups, and the leader of the CSU, Herbert Sorrell became a kind of folk hero to all those ordinary workers who were fighting the dictatorial methods of IATSE.

In 1943, the Set Decorators' Society joined the Painters and became part of the CSU. The producers refused to negotiate with the CSU, and despite a ruling by an arbitrator appointed by the War Labor Board that the producers should negotiate with the Painters, the producers continued to prevaricate. On 12 March 1945 the Painters went on strike and they were immediately supported by the other CSU unions. Four however did not. They were the Screen Publicists, the Office Employees, the Cartoonists and Story Analysts. They were influenced by the communists whose policy was one of no strikes during the war. The *People's World*, the Communist Party paper in Hollywood, ran an editorial which, although it blamed the producers for the strike, urged a back-to-work movement and accused Sorrell of being 'a good guy gone wrong'.

The very day that the CSU called its strike, a new IATSE organizer arrived in Hollywood. He was Roy Brewer who had been appointed by the new IATSE president, Richard Walsh. Brewer had been working with the War Labor Board in Washington and within two weeks of arriving in Hollywood IATSE began issuing daily bulletins attacking the CSU and the strikers. At first 'communism' was hardly mentioned, but very soon, Sorrell and the CSU were being pilloried day in and day out as 'communists'. Meanwhile the Communist Party were still opposing the strike, and IATSE was providing replacement labour to cross CSU picket lines.

With the ending of the war, the Communist Party changed its position and joined the CSU strike. Charily, the CSU welcomed their support, but on 5 October 1945, tear gas and fire hoses were used to break up a mass picket line at Warner Brothers studio. The AFL executive ordered a return to work, re-employment of all strikers, local negotiations for 30 days on inter-union disputes and a final settlement by a three-man committee of the AFL executive council on any questions unresolved after 30 days.

Nothing was really resolved by this process. Nobody was satisfied with the outcome and most liberals and progressives in Hollywood were outspokenly hostile to Brewer and IATSE. Sorrell and the CSU were regarded as honest and progressive. It was in this climate that Brewer began to associate with the virulently anti-communist Motion Picture Alliance for the Preservation of American Ideals, which had close links with the House Committee for Un-American Activities. Following an abortive intervention by the CSU in May 1946 over the Machinists Union which was no longer in the AFL, Brewer succeeded in getting the Los Angeles Central Labor Council to charge Sorrell with being a communist. The chief prosecutor was Ed Gibbons who had helped Brewer to prepare the anti-communist leaflets in the 1945 strike and who went on to become a co-owner of *Alert*, a 'nationalist' paper published in Los Angeles. Sorrell denied the charges against him and his trial faded out inconclusively.

Meanwhile there was a further CSU strike. This one was another jurisdictional question – and this time it was the Carpenters. The producers decided to sack all CSU members who refused to work on sets built by IATSE members. There were mass picketing and mass arrests every day. Finally the Roman Catholic Archbishop of Los Angleles assigned two priests to study the situation. They recommended that permanent arbitration machinery be set up with an impartial chairman. They criticized the studio heads for their 'most negative' attitude towards the strike and concluded among other things that 'the strike is not communist-inspired nor communist-dominated. It is also unfortunate that the CSU has turned again and again to left-wing sympathizers' support. But to desire the extermination of a union because of an accusation of communism is not in keeping with the facts nor with the spirit of labour ethics'.

CSU membership decreased and CSU members began to return to work with IATSE cards. Roy Brewer was in a position of great industrial as well as political strength. He went on to play a decisive role in the second investigation of Hollywood by the House Committee for Un-American Activities between 1951 and 1954. It was he who enabled many Hollywood writers, directors and stars to get off the unofficial blacklist and be re-employed in the studios. In order to clear themselves, they had to confess to any former associations with the Communist Party or its activities, to renounce them and, in addition, give evidence against any former associates whom they knew to have communist associations. Only when they had done this, would Brewer agree to persuade the studios to re-employ them. His co-operation with the studio bosses on industrial and political questions during the troublesome period between 1945 and 1949 meant that the studios were usually prepared to accede to his requests. Brewer was riding high. In 1949, he stood for election against Richard Walsh as President of IATSE, but lost. He immediately became an executive for Allied Artists. His move from labour to capital was complete.

The long and bitter struggle between the producers and IATSE on the one hand, and the FMPC, then the USTG, and finally the CSU on the other, was a reflection of fundamentally different perceptions of the industrial process and the autonomy of labour organizing its own activities and representing its own interests. What the Hollywood studio bosses wanted, and here they were supported by IATSE, was a system of management in which every worker, of whichever craft or grade, had to work according to a pattern and a plan which was decided at the top and then organized according to the principles of scientific management. In a large studio turning out over 50 feature films per year, most workers were simply regarded as factory hands. Only a few could be regarded as creative workers, whose organization will be looked at in the next chapter. When the various crafts or grades tried to organize themselves on a freer, more collective basis, they met with the combined opposition of the producers and IATSE. They were also the target of a barrage of hostile anti-communist propaganda, most of which was misplaced.

Fortunately the tensions between these two different models of industrial organization never surfaced in Great Britain in the violent form they took in Hollywood. The main reason for this was the different circumstances surrounding the origins of trade union organization in the British studios. Prior to the 1930s, trade union organization only really existed in the cinemas. A group of projectionists had formed the National Association of Cinematograph Operators (NACO) in 1906 and from the beginning it was associated with the National Association of Theatrical Employees (NATE), which organized backstage workers in the theatre. As the cinemas developed the need evolved for the projectionists to organize alongside other cinema workers as many cinemas became individually owned. The NATE leadership favoured co-operation with the employers rather than militancy and openly stated that their policy was to prevent strikes. A number of projectionists began to defect to the Electrical Trades Union (ETU), which was more militant that NATE. This brought about a long and bitter dispute between NATE and the ETU over the organization of projectionists, only resolved in 1947. But the dispute affected the film studios only marginally, for until 1933 most studio workers were unorganized.

The initial impetus for trade union organization in the film studios began at the Gaumont British studios at Shepherd's Bush where the head of production, Michael Balcon, had a policy of employing university-educated people as assistant directors and editors. Many of them were not only progressive in their politics, but they were generally appalled at the working conditions throughout the industry where workers were expected to work for 16 hours a day for seven days a week churning out low budget quota quickies. These vague aspirations went no further until Captain Cope an energetic gentleman who ran a 'health and strength' cafe in Shepherd's Bush market agreed to become unpaid organizer of the fledgling Association of Studio Workers (ASW). Cope soon renamed the ASW calling it the Association of Cinematograph Technicians (ACT – ACTT in the mid-1950s).

The new-born ACT was run from Cope's cafe in Shepherd's Bush market, but Cope's old-school approach to trade union organization was not regarded as effective and he soon resigned under pressure from the members committee led by Thorold Dickinson and J. Neill-Brown. Within 48 hours a new general secretary, George Elvin, had been appointed, and he was to remain secretary until 1969 when he was elected president on his retirement. The strategy of ACTT was to organize all grades from film director down to clapper loader. More significantly from an industrial point of view, it also decided to organize the laboratory workers. The laboratory workers were the working-class base of an essentially middle-class union, and when all the studios and production companies, with the notable exception of Gaumont British, refused to negotiate with the fledgling ACTT, it required a stern strike warning from ACT's laboratory workers at the time of George VI's coronation to bring them to the negotiating table.

The tensions between the two organizational models for film production which split the American trade unions in Hollywood never emerged in Britain because they were all effectively contained within the interfactional struggles which were fought out within the ACT, and in particular within its feature film branch. For several years the branch was organized both on a company basis, where members elected representatives according to their work place, but also on a craft or grade basis, according to qualification. Broadly speaking, the key ACT members in skilled grades, such as the art directors and the sound recordists, placed a strong emphasis on apprenticeship entry schemes and a firm control over the organization of labour within their own particular sections. The less skilled grades were happy to be organized according to the plans of the studio, provided of course, that they were not overworked. In addition, for historical reasons, certain grades such as the electricians were organized by the Electrical Trades Union (ETU), others such as make-up artists, hairdressers and studio projectionists were organized by NATE which had now become the National Association of Theatrical and Kinematograph Employees (NATKE).

The grave danger from the point of view of the film studios, and it was also one perceived by IATSE in Hollywood, was that if unions were allowed to organize on a craft basis they could disrupt the overall pattern of film production management. While the main concern of the studios was to prevent any economic disruption to film production, another concern was to maintain a firm political ideological control over film content, particularly when film technicians were expected to work on films which were inimical to their own political and ideological interests. An illustration of these tensions is to be found in the struggles which took place during the production of the propaganda feature film made for the Ministry of Information (MOI) by Two Cities Films, *The Demi-Paradise* (Anthony Asquith, 1943).

During the Second World War the MOI was faced with a tricky ideological and political problem when the Soviet Union joined Britain and her allies in her struggle against fascism in June 1941, six months before the US entered the war. It had to present the Soviet Union to the British people as an ally, but at the same time play down, or indeed camouflage, the fact that it was a communist country. 'I think it would be a mistake to make our main-effort criticism destructive of Soviet ideology,' wrote Sir Walter Monckton, Director General of the MOI, to his minister, Brendan Bracken, in September 1941. 'It would be better to throw up in positive contrast the enduring value of our own democratic way of political life.'

The production of *The Demi-Paradise* was part of the MOI's propaganda strategy. It was produced and partly scripted by the anti-communist Russian emigré producer, Anatole de Grunwald. Laurence Olivier was released from the armed forces by the MOI to star in the film as Ivan Kouznetsoff, an enthusiastic young Soviet engineer who invents a new type of propeller and who is sent to England to get it manufactured using the best British skills. During the production of the film however, the Denham Works Comittee objected to the number of scenes in the film which they felt prejudiced British relations with Russia. In particular, they objected to a scene in which Kouznetsoff takes time off from vital war work to get drunk in a pub. Both Anthony Asquith, director of the film and president of ACT, and the manager of Denham studios, objected strongly to the attempt of the Denham Works Committee to concern itself with the propaganda content of the film, but the Works Committee were supported by the General Council of the ACT. A few weeks later at ACT's Annual General Meeting Anthony Asquith objected to the decisions of its General Council, but the meeting supported the General Council and Anthony Asquith resigned. At the AGM, the ACT's General Secretary, George Elvin, read out a letter from Ivan Maisky the Soviet ambassador in London which declared that, 'the Soviet Embassy does not approve of the scenario in its present form and I am sorry to say that the Soviet Embassy would have no other choice but to protest against its showing.'

This was a perhaps a unique occasion when film technicians who were not working in the creative grades, were able to influence the content of the films on which they were working. One of the reasons for this was that technicians who worked at Denham film studios were employed on a permanent basis by Denham studios rather than on a freelance basis by Two Cities Films, the production company. Today, however, the advent of television and the changes in the marketplace for cinema films means that crews for nearly all films are employed on a freelance basis. Few technicians can now afford to jeopardize their future employment opportunities by objecting to the political and ideological content of films on which they work. Consequently, the people who influence the content of films are the key creative grades – the producers, writers, directors and performers – and it is to them and the way in which their labour is organized that we must now turn.

6. Creativity

Film, it is frequently argued, is an art form. If so, where does the creative control lie? In its earliest days film was seen as an extension of photography. The film director was merely an assistant to help the cameraman compose his picture, and to tell the actors when and where to move. In the United States, when D.W. Griffith started directing at Biograph in 1908, his chief cameraman, Billy Bitzer, was gradually eased out of creative control while Griffith took charge of both the script supervision and the direction of the actors. When they filmed on location, it was normal to set up the camera in a position which offered some shade to both the camera and the cameraman. This frequently determined the background of the shot concerned. To get the cameraman out of the shade, Griffith had to resort to subterfuge. On one occasion he sent out for some bottled beer, and dangled it enticingly over the spot where he wanted the new camera set up. For one bottle Bitzer looked interested, for two he would move.

However, the struggles for creative control were not always so gentlemanly. Filming at Biograph was a protected occupation, because films made there were largely financed by the royalties the company received from its stockholdings in the Motion Picture Patents Company, which collectively held all the patent rights to cameras and projectors. Film revenues were not linked as directly to their commercial success in the marketplace as they were for those companies whose industrial structure was based on film copyright. There, as we have seen, an alternative form of organization was developed on the principles of scientific management. Under this system creative control was centred in the hands of the film producer, not the film director.

The division of labour was an essential factor in maintaining creative control over film-making, as the young Irving Thalberg found out when he was assistant to Carl Laemmele, the head of

Universal Studios. Left in charge by Laemmele, Thalberg discovered that Erich von Stroheim who was directing and starring in *Foolish Wives* was running over schedule and over budget and, in Thalberg's opinion, wasting time and money on unnecessarily self-indulgent shooting. Thalberg tried to take von Stroheim off the picture and to substitute a new director, but discovered he was powerless, for if von Stroheim ceased to direct, he also ceased to star and the picture could not be finished without him.

The classic system of the division of labour thus attempted, insofar as it was possible, to relegate the director to the position of supervisor, responsible only for the supervision of the actors and the camera crew, and turning the shooting script into daily rushes. The set designs and the costumes were all approved in advance by the producer, the camera crew had its instructions to conform to the visual style of the studio, the stars and the actors were chosen by the casting department of the studio, and no sets were to be struck until the producer had personally approved the rushes. When he was head of production at MGM, Thalberg rejected so many directors' rushes at MGM's Culver City studios in the San Fernando Valley that the area became known as 'retake valley'.

The major studios also developed their systems for controlling the creative freedom of the scriptwriters, the stars and the editors. The relationship between a script and a scriptwriter was not regarded as sacrosanct. To be a scriptwriter at the big studios was more akin to working in a factory than to being an author or a playwright. Scriptwriters were expected to clock in and clock off, and scripts were frequently transferred from one writer to another if the producer didn't approve of the drafts. Some writers were simply employed as specialist writers for their expertise in writing action scenes, gags, love scenes or whatever, and they were expected to write scenes for films in which they had no previous involvement. This was the division of labour as applied to scriptwriting.

Film stars were of course a key ingredient in a film's success at the box office. The form of agreement between the studios and the stars was a trade-off known as the studio contract. According to its terms, the star was paid a very substantial salary in return for total compliance with the wishes of the studio. Stars were employed on conditions which, as Sir William Jowitt KC was to argue before the High Court in London in 1936, made his client, Bette Davis, a mere chattel of Warner Bros. 'Slavery,' he went on to argue, 'is not the less slavery because the chains are gilded.'

The terms and conditions of the contract which the star was required to sign with the studio made him or her the exclusive property of the studio. S/he was not allowed to work for any other producer until the contract expired. Contracts normally ran for one year, but also built into the contract was the right of the studio to renew the contract for up to seven years, a right not normally granted to the star. Furthermore, if the star misbehaved in any way, the studio had the right to put the star on suspension until s/he started to behave in the required manner, and the contract was automatically extended for the period of suspension. The studios developed their contract system from that used to employ baseball players, but the ways in which they deployed it went much further. Good behaviour, according to the studios, meant that the star had to appear in every role which the studio chose, to act and behave off set and in private life in a manner which the studio deemed fitting to the image it wanted to convey to the public, and to consent to participate in whatever publicity activities the studio deemed desirable. In return, the star was normally paid a basic salary when not working, which was substantially increased whenever s/he appeared in a picture.

The aim of the studios was to blend the image of the star, the role played in a succession of films, and the persona of the star as portrayed by the studio publicity department and the gossip columnists. A great deal of time and effort was given over to this. Scripts were chosen, written even, to act as vehicles for the star concerned. In the early days, before the studios mastered the contract system, the stars had a lot of economic power, and many of them deployed this in order to get scripts written which portrayed the stars as they saw themselves. But as the studios mastered the contract system during the 1930s, creative control swung back to the studios. The stars became 'the powerless elite'.

With the break-up of the studio system during the 1950s, stars began to have more creative freedom to control their own image, and to appear in films of their own choosing. Stars such as Gregory Peck, Paul Newman, John Wayne and Jane Fonda have all used their economic power to build their images in a way which reflects their own personalities. Others such as Grace Kelly and Marilyn Monroe were products of the old studio system. MGM assiduously cultivated an image of Grace Kelly as cool, genteel, elegant and reserved by planting feature material in women's magazines which emphasized her family's good life, augmented by quotes from co-stars concerning her off-screen ladylike qualities. On the other hand, Twentieth Century Fox released numerous pin-up photographs of Marilyn Monroe, emphasizing her pre-Hollywood experience as a pin-up and cover girl for men's magazines. Feature material on her was released to men's magazines rather than women's magazines. If Kelly was the ideal mate for Eisenhower's America, Monroe was its ideal playmate. And since life imitates fantasy, Grace Kelly went on to become the wife of Prince Rainier of Monaco, Marilyn Monroe to become the lover of President Kennedy of America.

The role of the director in the struggle for the creative control of films has also changed with the times. While working for Biograph between 1908 and 1913, D.W. Griffith created a distinct visual style which was recognized by critics and audiences alike. But during his years at Biograph he was working in a protected enclave, shielded from the demands of the marketplace by Biograph's profits from its patent rights. When he left Biograph his career flourished briefly with the racist *Birth of a Nation* and then steadily declined into critical success but commercial failure.

For the studios the director was an artist who was out of touch with the marketplace and he was downgraded in the new division of labour which followed the implementation of scientific management by the new vertically integrated corporations. This stood in direct contrast to the totally different method of organizing film production which was developed in Weimar Germany and which was Hollywood's main rival for the world market during the 1920s. The economics of production in Weimar Germany were totally different from those of Hollywood. In Hollywood film stock was relatively cheap and the studio chiefs could afford to require a director to reshoot a scene several times until it was done properly. In Germany on the other hand, film negative was extremely expensive since it had to be paid for in foreign currency and since, during the period between the end of the First World War and Germany's return to the gold standard in November 1923, there was massive inflation with the German mark being devalued almost daily. This meant that the economics of film production were turned upside down. The German studios could afford human labour but not photographic material. Directorial efficiency was therefore at a premium, and every scene had to be carefully pre-planned so that, whenever possible, it could be shot in one take. This in turn meant that a great deal of creative autonomy was given to the director, the actors and their colleagues in the camera and art departments. As a result the films produced had a distinctly different appearance and were strongly influenced by contemporary expressionist painting and parallel developments in literature and drama.

The instability of the German mark against the dollar and the gold standard provided additional reasons for the development of this 'expressionist' film style. Profits from the German domestic market only accounted for 10 per cent of the production costs of German films, the other 90 per cent had to come from overseas. To this end the films were designed to achieve critical acclaim in New York, in London and in Paris, where they showed a marked product differentiation from Hollywood's mass-oriented films. Measured in dollars, pounds sterling or French francs, their earnings may have been modest, but measured in German rentenmarks they were substantial.

The advent of talking pictures in 1927 meant that Hollywood had to invest large sums of money in building sound stages. But increased capital investments required increased profits, and in a collapsing market triggered by the Wall Street crash, Hollywood found that it was having to reassess the economic efficiency of its studios. A trade-off had to be organized between creative control and economic efficiency, and as the German experience had shown, it was the director who tended to take creative control. Hollywood was reluctant to change its old profligate ways. In the decade between 1927 and 1937 the number of films produced in Hollywood fell by approximately one-third, but the number of producers increased nearly sevenfold, while the number of directors remained approximately constant. The chain of command between the studio head and the individual directors was not only becoming longer but increasingly ineffective. By the middle of the decade, however, individual directors such as John Ford, King Vidor, Rouben Mamoulian, Frank Capra, Josef von Sternberg and Fritz Lang were all beginning to make their mark as individual stylists.

Directors were beginning to bridge the gap between mental and manual labour. Hollywood was forced to realize that it made both economic and artistic sense for the writer and the director to work together on the script before it went on the studio floor and certain producers such as the independent Sam Goldwyn and the MGM-based Arthur Freed began to encourage creative and collaborative teamwork. These practices occurred more naturally at the quality end of Hollywood's product, since like any other industry, the industry liked to turn out what it saw as a product mix, producing films at different budgets designed to appeal to different sectors of the market. In 1927 Jesse Lasky told a seminar at the Harvard Business School that there were basically three types of picture: the programme picture that was not expected to run longer than a week; what Lasky called 'Rialto specials' which were designed to run as long as the public would patronize them; and a few road show pictures which were produced to bring goodwill and prestige to the studios rather than to make profits. Indeed many of them made a loss, but the studios judged that their production costs were money well spent since they brought critical approval and the patronage of the increasingly articulate and politically powerful middle class. The division of a studio's output was paralleled by a similar change in the organization of the work process, with the director being given more creative freedom in the prestige picture. Many of the directors who established their reputation early were directors of prestige pictures such as King Vidor at MGM, Josef von Sternberg at Paramount and Frank Capra at Columbia.

In Great Britain, production was a far less organized affair than in Hollywood, and films were made in a more artisanal manner. The only serious rival to Hollywood in the 1930s was Alexander Korda's Denham studios. Here it was not so much organization as extravagance which seemed to dominate the scene. The majority of the creative personnel were usually German or other central European refugees from Hitler, and the German mode of production was very influential at Denham in the 1930s.

The one significant contribution to production organization that was made by British studios was the system devised by Michael Balcon at Ealing studios between 1939 and 1955. Drawing on the studio motto, 'the studio with the team spirit', which had been introduced by his predecessor and the founder of the studio, Basil Dean, Balcon gathered round him a team of hand-picked young men who worked together in teams of three – scriptwriter, associate producer and director – and who exchanged ideas, comments and criticisms with other creative teams at regular round table conferences which Balcon organized in the studio. Balcon was very careful in choosing those whom he admitted to his creative elite. They were all selected to ensure that they had broadly the same world view as he did, they were all young and depended on his patronage to be promoted to positions of creative power, and they were only allowed to start work on subjects which had his approval. Balcon was able to negotiate a protected position for the studio and its products within the protective umbrella of the Rank Organization, and it was in this way that the studio was able to survive for so long despite the failure of many of its films.

Not surprisingly there was a remarkable consistency in the films which came out of Ealing studios. The collective method of production and the care with which Balcon selected the members of his creative elite to reflect his own world view ensured that his presence showed in all the films that came out of the studio. Although it is possible to identify the marks of individual creative personalities such as the scriptwriter T.E.B. Clarke, or the directors Robert Hamer or Alexander Mackendrick, these are but minor variations on Ealing's recurring theme that human nature is basically good and that the fundamental decency and good will latent in all classes of British society will pull us through in the end, in peacetime as well as in war.

The careful development of a team spirit which was the hallmark of the way Ealing's creative elite was organized, was not shared by its rival studio working within the Rank organization – Gainsborough. There economy and efficiency played a central role. During its heyday between 1936 and 1948 it was organized like a miniature version of a Hollywood studio. Under the watchful eye of the studio head Maurice Ostrer, his key producers, first Ted Black and later R.J. Minney and Harold Huth, set out to build a stable of popular British stars and to produce popular films specially designed for the tastes of the British public. The most sucessful of these were the costume melodramas, adapted from bestselling historical romantic novels, produced between 1943 and 1947. Examples are *Madonna of the Seven Moons* (Arthur Crabtree, 1944) and *The Wicked Lady* (Leslie Arliss, 1945). Gainsborough's stars such as Margaret Lockwood, James Mason, Stewart Granger and Phyllis Calvert, outshone even the big Hollywood stars at the British box office but, unlike Ealing's films which gained critical approval, Gainsborough's films were disliked by the critical elite.

The drive for economy and efficiency at Gainsborough – some called it meanness – meant that there was little central control over the art direction and costume departments. The main creative thrust came from R.J. Minney and his scriptwriters such as Margaret Kennedy, Leslie Arliss and Roland Pertwee, and although Maurice Ostrer demanded a 'cast-iron script' before shooting started, the studio practice was for writers to change the scripts at the last minute as the rushes came in. Frequently the modifications would have to take account of the different 'look' of the rushes brought about by the fact that there was little time for liaison between the scriptwriters and the art direction and costume departments.

Minney's view was that in an ideal world the scriptwriter should also direct the film. Certainly a close working relationship between the two grades is essential for a film which is to have its own artistic coherence, but this form of liaison sat uneasily with the form of studio organization employed both at Gainsborough and in Hollywood. The break-up of the studio system as the mass audience switched from the cinema to television meant, however, that the balance of forces between economic efficiency and creative coherence changed. Today the director is normally thought of as being the dominant creative force in films produced for the cinema since they are normally made on a one-off basis. In television series however, whether they are made in Hollywood for US television, or whether they are shot in Britain by the British television organizations, it is the series producers and the script editors who are the real centres of creative power, not the directors.

The division of labour within the Hollywood studios had a key effect on the structure and organization of labour organizations there. When Hollywood signed the studio basic agreement in 1926, it left out of the agreement all of the key creative grades. Accordingly, the following year it set up the Academy of Motion Picture Arts and Sciences (AMPAS) as an employee representation organization. AMPAS had five sections, one for producers, one for scriptwriters and one for directors. The fourth was for actors and actresses and the fifth was for key technical personnel such as lighting cameramen and special effects technicians. The basic idea was that the Academy would contain the legitimate demands of the workers it claimed to represent, rather than to pursue them with vigour.

Without much difficulty AMPAS secured a minimum standard contract for actors and actress and a grievance procedure, but its bargaining activities didn't go much further. It became more like a senior staff club, and the following year organized the 'Oscar' ceremonies which were designed to encourage members to compete against one another in the pursuit of excellence, rather than to act collectively in each other's interests. The collapse of the US economy following the Wall Street crash, the depression and the bank moratorium in March 1933, left the Academy bereft of any policy for its members except to recommend 50 per cent salary cuts for eight weeks. Naturally the members who were highest paid, such as the writers and the actors, suffered the most, a procedure which didn't conform to Hollywood's self-image at all. It was the highest paid who led the walk-out from the Academy, effectively leaving only the Oscar ceremonies which still survive today as a piece of highly commercialized razzmatazz.

The actors and the writers were able to lead a walk-out because the advent of talking pictures had brought a substantial influx of talented writers and actors from Broadway. There had been a strike by Equity, the actors union, for recognition in 1929, which had been supported by a large number of Broadway actors working in Hollywood, but it had failed. The following year Roosevelt's New Deal administration tried to put together a code of fair practice for the film industry under the aegis of the National Recovery Administration. The studios wanted the Academy to represent the talent groups and to prevent actors, writers and directors switching from one studio to another without studio approval. Both the Screen Actors' Guild (SAG) and the Screen Writers' Guild (SWG) were formed in opposition to this. Intense lobbying of President Roosevelt by Eddie Cantor, President of the Screen Actors Guild, got the proposal withdrawn.

In 1935 the National Recovery Administration was declared unconstitutional by the Supreme Court and the Wagner Act was introduced to regulate labour relations. The new act provided for an election within one industry or profession when there were competing unions. SAG was recognized by the producers in May 1937 and they were guaranteed a 54-hour week dropping to 48 hours the following year.

In the field of scriptwriting there was a constant struggle between the Screen Playwrights (SP, a right-wing organization consisting mainly of writers who had worked for silent films and who were supported by the studios), and the younger SWG, comprised mainly of writers for talkies and those who were dissatisfied with the Academy. The National Labour Relations Board organized an election in August 1938 which the SWG won. They were recognized in 1940 and established a contract which guaranteed a minimum wage, banned the practice of writers being asked to write on a speculative basis without any guarantee of payment if their material was not used, and which allowed the SWG to decide which writers should be given the scriptwriting credit on a film – a particularly important matter in Hollywood where nobody really knew who did what on each individual script.

The Screen Directors' Guild was not formed until 1936 and it took it a further three years to obtain recognition. Once achieved, it negotiated greater freedom for its members, including the right to work with writers on the film scripts. Times were changing in Hollywood. The centre of gravity was moving away from the studio boss towards the scriptwriter and the director. One little-noticed provision in the agreement which the studios signed with the SWG in May 1940 was that it provided for an 85 per cent closed shop until 1948, to be followed thereafter by a 90 per cent shop.

The advent of the Second World War reduced the inter-organizational struggles between writers' organizations to relative insignificance, but two activists of the now defunct Screen Playwrights resurfaced in the virulent anti-communist Motion Picture Alliance for the Preservation of American Ideals (MPAPAI). The possibility of 90 per cent closed shop in Hollywood, combined with the gradual erosion of the creative control of the studio bosses, meant that once again the latter had common cause with the former activists in the SP against the SWG. Jack Warner and Louis B. Mayer appeared alongside the MPAPAI as friendly witnesses when the House Committee for Un-American Activities took evidence in Hollywood for the first time in October 1947. Of the ten film workers who were blacklisted, eight were writers, all of them activists in the SWG.

The Hollywood moguls repaired to the Waldorf Astoria from which they emerged on 24 November issuing a declaration that the Hollywood Ten had been a 'disservice to their employers' and suspended them without compensation. More ominously they then asked the Hollywood talent guilds to help them eliminate the subversives in their ranks. By deploying the Cold War rhetoric of anti-communism, the Hollywood moguls were attempting to regain some form of creative control over the content of their films, while at the same time attempting to purge the guilds of activists. The anti-communist rhetoric was deployed both by the studio bosses against the talent guilds and by the IATSE against the unions affiliated to the Confederation of Studio Unions. The threat of the blacklist hung like a pall over any creative activity in Hollywood for the next decade. Many of Hollywood's most creative directors and writers such as Carl Foreman and Joseph Losey, left to make films elsewhere, frequently in Great Britain where the ideological climate was more liberal.

The organization of labour in Great Britain benefited because when the ACT was formed in 1933 the assistant directors and editors, many of whom were working at the Shepherd's Bush studios of Gaumont British and had been university educated. ACT set out therefore to organize all grades from director downwards. Its president from 1937, Anthony Asquith, was a distinguished director and the split between the industrial unions and the talent guilds which appeared in Hollywood did not appear within the British trade unions for some time. Problems started to arise however with the organization of

scriptwriters. In March 1937 a number of scriptwriters, including writers at Gainsborough such as R.J.Minney, Leslie Arliss,
Frank Launder, Sidney Gilliat, Margaret Kennedy and Roland
Pertwee, founded the Screenwriters' Association (SWA). The
ACT also claimed to organize writers, but its strength lay in the
documentary field rather than the feature field. The philosophy
of the SWA was closer to that of a guild than a trade union and it
firmly rejected ACT's claim to organize writers. They saw
themselves, said screen writer Frank Launder, as being 'neither
reactionary conservatives nor reactionary unionists, but just
simple, progressive benevolent anarchists'. By 1947 they had
become the Screenwriters Guild and were acting as a trade
union in opposition to the ACT.

The screenwriters' view of themselves as 'simple benevolent
anarchists' appeared to ignore the fact that it was normally the
studios and the companies taking the financial risks of film
production which decided which projects to film. Therefore
writers were chosen as much for their political and ideological
values as for their skills as wordsmiths. The protected milieu
within which many of the SWA activists had worked at
Gainsborough was soon to disappear. No doubt too, there were
many writers who saw themselves as superior to ordinary film
technicians and who were appalled at the support given to the
Denham Works Committee by the ACT's General Council and
by its Annual General Meeting when it became concerned about
the propaganda implications of the original script of *The Demi-
Paradise*. The relationship between industrial organization and
creative activity in film production has changed and altered
according to the time and the situation concerned. When
Hollywood was in its industrial heyday, the studio bosses saw
the progressive unionization of Hollywood as a threat not only to
its economic viability but also to their control over the
organization of the creative talent working for them. Paradoxi-
cally perhaps, the studio boss who felt this most keenly was Jack
L. Warner at Warner Brothers, for the latter had a reputation for
being one of the most progressive studios in Hollywood and,
according to a survey carried out in 1940, the one which writers
respected most. Warner's had built their reputation on making
films with contemporary subject matter drawn from real-life
newspaper stories. Warner's also had very close links with

President Roosevelt and were strong supporters of his New Deal policy, making films like *Forty-Second Street* (Lloyd Bacon, 1933) at the time of his inauguration as President and *Mission to Moscow* (Michael Curtiz, 1943) when the White House needed the Russians as allies during the Second World War. Whether Warner was so hostile both to the activities of the CSU and to the SWG because he felt he had left himself open to the charge of being 'soft' on communism, or whether it was because he felt intellectually inferior to many of the writers working in his studio is not clear. What is clear is that he felt that the establishment of a 90 per cent closed shop for scriptwriters threatened not only the economic base on which the studio was run, but also his ability to employ new writers who were not only cheap but would write the sort of scripts that he and his senior producers wanted – whether to suit the needs of the box office or of his political associates. Warner's attack on the 'communists' in Hollywood, which terrified all the liberals who were able to work there, was one of the most virulent of all the studio bosses. The similar attacks which were launched by Louis B. Mayer, the long-time Republican head of MGM were less surprising, if no less disturbing.

The concern over the ways in which the industrial organization of scriptwriters might affect the content of the films made by the film studios was echoed in Great Britain in the struggle which took place over which organization was to represent the interests of scriptwriters – the SWA or the ACT. The SWA activists, many of them working at Gainsborough, wanted to be non-industrial and 'free' and were either unable or unwilling to recognize that the creative freedom which they enjoyed came not from some mystical human right, but rather from the fact that their creative abilities coincided with the industrial needs of Gainsborough film studios. When the SWA finally became a fully-fledged organization, it became first the Television and Screenwriters Guild and later the Writers Guild of Great Britain.

The conviction of the talent grades that they needed a guild rather than a trade union was shared by their colleagues in Hollywood. Guildism offered a rhetoric of supporting their individual creative freedom, but it ignored the fact that some of their members were economically far more successful than others and that it was the employers who decided which of their members to employ at high salaries and which to reject. The guilds only deployed the collective strength of their members on very rare occasions and remained organizationally aloof from the industrial base of studio production on which their wealth was built.

The fear shared by the studio bosses in Hollywood and by some of the activists in the SWA that unionization would limit their creative freedom, was in reality largely unfounded. It was only within the heavily industrialized environment of the Hollywood studio in its heyday that collective action over a film's content might have been possible, and even there most studio workers accepted Hollywood's basic ideology of hard work leading to happiness and success.

Once the cinema ceased to be *the* mass medium, and yielded ground to television, the problem was no longer so acute. Individual producers were able to pick and choose the writer or the director they wanted from a casualized freelance market and these in turn could be related to the creative and ideological needs of the distributor, the senior studio executive or the bank which was providing the principal source of finance for the film. In television, however, which still commanded the mass market audience, a different form of organization prevailed. There the dominant fictional form was the television series. The script-writers were employed on a freelance basis, a philosophy which suited the guilds and the television organizations perfectly, for creative control remained with the series producer, the script editor and ultimately the network.

Today, however, the outlook for creative film-makers is improving. The collapse of the Hollywood studio system, the increasing involvement of television organizations in film financing and the growing demand of new markets for new films, now means that the balance of supply and demand between the need for new films and the availability of creative talent is beginning to tilt in favour of the film-maker. The talented have the opportunity to make films that say what they want to say, albeit in a limited way, as opposed to what the distributor or studio wants them to say.

7. Protection

The importance of film and the need to protect the domestic film industry against Hollywood domination has been recognized by national governments for many decades. The debate in Great Britain, where the film industry shares a common language with that of Hollywood, has been particularly confused as industrial and artistic arguments have become hopelessly entwined.

The first substantial piece of legislation to protect the British film industry was introduced by a Conservative government in 1927. The pressure for legislative intervention had come from the Federation of British Industries, since neither the cinema exhibitors nor the film distributors favoured legislative change that might threaten the profits they made from showing Hollywood films in Britain, and since the few remaining film producers were so weak as to be politically ineffective. The move was also resisted by sections of the Labour Party who saw the cinema as the principal form of working-class entertainment and suspected the Tories of wanting to replace popular and classless Hollywood films with British films saturated with class snobbery and Tory values.

Protectionist legislation for film production was part of a general philosophy of Conservative governments of the period. But the rhetoric with which the President of the Board of Trade introduced the new legislation to the House of Commons was substantially different. He stressed that, as the Hollywood experience had shown, cinema was 'the greatest advertising power in the world' and went on to ask rhetorically whether members of parliament would 'be content for a moment if we depended upon foreign literature or a foreign press in this country'. If the rhetoric was addressed to culture, the legislative reality was industrial protection in which concepts of quality were significantly absent from the legislative provisions. What the new Act required was that both cinema exhibitors and film distributors should show and offer for rent an increasing proportion of British films each year. The exhibitors' quota was scheduled to rise from 5 per cent in 1929 to 20 per cent in 1936-39, and the renters' quota was to rise from 7.5 per cent to 20 per cent during the same period. There were also provisions designed to eliminate the worst American trade practices such as blind, block and advance booking of films into cinemas. No film could be distributed until it had been registered with the Board of Trade, and no film could be registered until it had been trade shown to exhibitors.

The Act defined a British film as one which was made by a British company, which used a film studio located in the British Empire and which had a British subject as the author of the scenario. Finally, not less than 75 per cent of labour costs, (excluding copyright payments and the salary of one foreign actor, actress or producer) were to be paid to residents of the British Empire. Not surprisingly therefore, the American companies exploited the deficiencies in the act either by setting up production subsidiaries to fulfil their quota requirements as cheaply as possible, or by subcontracting their production requirements to compliant 'independent' British producers. The majority of British films produced during the 1930s were 'quota quickies' which employed British technicians but were often shown to empty cinemas in the early hours of the morning when only the cleaners were in the cinema. These films were budgeted at around £1.00 per foot of film projected, that is between £6,000 and £7,500 per film depending on length.

The outcome of the 1927 Act was not wholly bad, however. The growth in the market for quota quickies provided an environment where young, but exploited, film-makers such as Michael Powell and Thorold Dickinson could develop their talents. But despite the odd pockets of resistance such as the work of the Marxist director, Bernhard Vorhaus, and John Baxter, the socialist director who was trying to build on the working-class traditions of the music hall, the content of British films of the 1930s was largely imitative of Hollywood. Even the work of the lavish Hungarian-born impressario, Alexander Korda, which recreated patriotic episodes in British history in films such as *The Private Life of Henry VIII*, and jingoistic and imperialist propaganda films such as *Sanders of the River* and *The Drum*, was essentially designed for the American marketplace through his financial tie-up with United Artists.

The one lasting progressive outcome of the 1927 Act was the one least expected by its Tory proponents. The poor working conditions and low salaries imposed on most film technicians led to the formation of the films technicians' trade union, ACT, which was to play a key role in shaping the 1938 Act which replaced the 1927 Act. Neither the 1927 Act, nor the first Bill for the 1938 Act contained any provision as to the wages which were to be paid to film technicians or to cinema staff. Accordingly the Film Industry Employees Council, led by ACT and their colleagues in NATE, arranged to lobby members of the Standing Committee considering the Films Bill. Some 200 unemployed film technicians visited the Houses of Parliament to point out that around 80 per cent of the workers engaged in film production were unemployed. Although the Metropolitan Police had given their consent for a meeting to be held at the foot of the Irving Statue in Charing Cross Road, they suddenly changed their minds and forbade the meeting, citing the Seditious Meetings Act of 1817 which had been passed as a piece of 'temporary' legislation to control protests about the massive unemployment, the high price of bread and the fact that there was no vote. One of the provisions of the 1817 Act was that no meeting should be held within one mile of the Houses of Parliament while they were in session. Accordingly the meeting had to be transferred to Gatti's Restaurant nearby. More importantly, however, the film workers' case was highlighted in the national press and the net outcome was that the campaign to amend the Bill led by the ex-miner and Labour MP, Tom Williams, was successful. The Act was amended to protect the wages and conditions of employment of film workers by requiring makers and processors of films to pay wages and provide conditions of employment no less favourable than those required to fulfil government contracts, which in turn required employers to pay wages and observe working conditions at least as favourable as those recognized in trade union agreements. Five months later film workers were given further protection when film studios were designated as factories, and studio workers were protected by the provisions of the Factories Act.

In the main debate surrounding the 1938 Films Act, however, the employers and the union were on the same side. A report by the Moyne Committee which had been set up by the government to report on the operation of the 1927 Act, was concerned at the lack of quality in British films. It recommended that a body be set up to determine whether or not films were of a suitable quality to be eligible for British quota. Not surprisingly this was opposed by all sections of the film trade. But the ACT was equally opposed to the proposal. The question of quality was by no means an uncontroversial issue. A far better criterion, ACT argued, was a cost criterion, since although an expensive film might lack entertainment qualities, and a cheap picture might on occasion prove extremely popular, the more expensive picture gave scope for technical excellence whereas a cheap film did not. The cost arguments won the day: quota films were to have minimum labour costs of £7,500 and of at least £1.00 per foot; films with labour costs between £22,500 and 37,500 and costing between £3.00 and £5.00 per foot were to be eligible for double quota; and films with labour costs greater than £37,500 and costing more than £5.00 per foot were to be eligible for treble quota.

The underlying rationale for these provisions was to encourage the American companies to invest substantial sums of money in British film production, which was just what the Americans had been pressing for in private through the London representative of the Hays Office, the US State Department, and Joseph Kennedy, a former film producer and the new US ambassador to London. In truth, as F.D. Klingender and Stuart Legg had shown in their book, *Money Behind the Screen*, published late in 1936, the British film industry was financially dependent on Hollywood. It was to Hollywood that the British government listened and the gains made by the Film Industry Employees Council were only possible because they did not conflict with Hollywood's long-term interests.

Before the 1938 Act had a chance to make much of an impact, Britain was embroiled in the Second World War, and dependence on America became even greater. At the beginning Britain needed American help to defeat the Nazis; and at the end, American money to finance the economic recovery. The prime concern of the Treasury at the outbreak of war was the substantial drain of sterling to the United States in payment for film rentals. Initially it was proposed to impose import restrictions, but the US ambassador resisted vigorously and insisted on being involved in any proposals affecting the film industry. The Treasury capitulated, and a voluntary agreement was negotiated with the Americans who agreed to limit the amount they took out of the British economy in film rentals to $17.5 million per year. The remainder of their revenues, approximately double that amount, was to remain in Great Britain.

The agreement was renegotiated annually until 1942 when America entered the war alongside Britain and Russia and all restrictions were removed. It was not until 1947 that the matter was taken up again, this time by a Labour Government. The Chancellor, Sir Hugh Dalton, announced a tax on imported film designed to absorb 75 per cent of the money leaving the country. The Motion Picture Export Association of America (MPEA) immediately reacted by blocking the flow of all films to Britain. Although there was a six month supply of films for British cinemas, the Labour government had to start negotiating with the MPEA almost immediately. Seven months later, in March 1948, an agreement was reached which was similar to that which the Treasury had negotiated in the early years of the war. The agreement which ran for two years, and which was extended for a further three years, limited the outflow of funds to $17 million per year plus an amount equivalent to the earnings of British films in America. The remaining rentals were to be retained for use in a range of closely defined ways to be supervised by a joint Anglo-US Control Committee. It was envisaged that the bulk of the unspent revenues would be spent within the film industry on the production of new films.

In 1948 it became necessary for the 1938 Films Act to be renewed. The only change of any significance was in the quota regulations. As a result of American pressure at the discussions setting up the General Agreement on Tariffs and Trade (GATT), Western countries were forbidden to have distributors' quotas in their domestic legislation. Exhibitor quotas were still permitted however. Accordingly the requirement for a distributors' quota of British films was dropped from the 1948 Act, and another hole was punched in the protective shield which the

British government had tried to set up for the British film industry. The gap was a major one, however, for it was the film distributors who dominated the film trade, and exhibitors were dependent on distributors for a regular supply of films for their screens. In these circumstances the protective device of the exhibitors' quota was only of marginal significance, as Harold Wilson discovered when he set the level for the exhibitors' quota at 45 per cent in the first year of the new Act. It was greeted with protest from both the Americans and the exhibitors. In the following year it was lowered to 40 per cent, and a year later to 30 per cent where it stayed for the next 30 years since this was a level which the trade felt it could achieve without undue commercial hardship.

By 1948 British policy was turning from one of building up an indigenous and independent British film industry to one of building up an industry which would conform to the interests of America. With the abolition of the renters' quota the only real restrictions which remained on the statute book were the provisions preventing blind, block and advance booking, and the fig leaf of an exhibitors' quota, meaningless anyway since the exhibitor who failed to meet it could always offer the defence that it was not commercially practicable to meet the quota. As a result no prosecution for breach of the quota ever succeeded and hardly any have ever been brought. Future developments in British film policy were therefore based on a policy of financial inducement rather than defensive protection.

The first step was the setting up in 1949 of the National Film Finance Corporation which was provided with a revolving fund of £5 million, increased to £6 million the following year, to finance British film production on a commercial basis. In its early years it lent large sums to Alexander Korda who lost nearly £3 million of its money on his production of *Bonnie Prince Charlie* before he went bankrupt. In order to keep financially solvent NFFC policy changed to one of co-operating with commercial film distributors in co-financing arrangements. A producer could normally raise about 70 per cent of his film finance against a distributor's guarantee, which was only made available on the condition that the distributor's portion was recouped before any of the other investors. The NFFC became the main source of the remaining 30 per cent of production finance, which was known as 'end money' since its investment was recouped last. Naturally, the extremely high financial risk involved in 'end money' investment meant that few, if any, private sector investors were prepared to participate on these terms. As a result, during the next two decades many films were financed which, according to the accountants, made a loss, but on which the commercial distributors made large profits. This occurred in two ways. The distributor would first take a substantial fee for distributing the film – normally 30 per cent – but would pass all print and advertising costs directly on to the producer. Secondly, the distributor would either recoup his 70 per cent 'front money' investment, along with the interest on the loan, or alternatively not be required to call on his guarantee. The 'end money' investor, on the other hand, normally the NFFC, could well find that the film, having had to bear all these substantial deductions 'up front' did not cover its production costs. In a disguised form therefore the NFFC was often acting as a hidden subsidizer of the commercial film distributors.

The second form of aid was the Eady Levy, named after the Treasury civil servant who helped to devise the scheme, Sir Wilfred Eady. The basis of the scheme was that there should be a levy on the cinema receipts of all films shown in Great Britain, both British and foreign. The money raised by this levy would then be redistributed to producers of British films, in proportion to their film rentals. The basic idea behind the scheme was that all films, but principally American films, would contribute to the levy, and neither the film renters nor the producers of foreign films would benefit. In this way, Hollywood would help to finance the production of British films.

The Eady Levy scheme was taken up by the film industry and organized by them on a voluntary basis. This had a number of advantages: it did not require the government to pass anti-American legislation ; the details of the scheme were acceptable to all sections of the British film industry; and the new scheme did not conflict with the rules of GATT. Crucial to the success of the scheme were the criteria for allocating the levy, since in order for the renters and the exhibitors to agree, the scheme had to encourage potentially profitable films and permit the major American companies to become 'producers of British films' so that they too might benefit from the levy. Finally, the government was persuaded to concede a reduction in entertainment tax when the voluntary levy scheme was introduced.

The important factors defining a British film, were that the film had to be made by a British company, it had to be shot in a British studio and a requisite proportion of labour costs had to be British. That requisite proportion was 75 per cent (excluding one person), or 80 per cent (excluding two people, one of whom had to be an actor or actress). These requirements were ones which the major American companies could live with and which allowed them to develop an international production strategy appropriate to the 1950s.

By the end of the 1940s Hollywood had found itself in a position which necessitated a different financial strategy from the one it had developed since 1920. That strategy had been one of developing high-cost mass production values and star appeal which would capture first the American market and then the world market. In this it had succeeded admirably, but the flow of production finance for these films could only be raised by using the real estate values of its cinemas in the big city centres as the security against which to raise the necessary loans from the banks. In 1947 the US Supreme Court handed down an anti-trust judgement which struck at the heart of Hollywood's financial structure. It decreed that Hollywood's exhibition interests were to be divorced form its distribution and production interests.

Other factors too were threatening Hollywood's position as the dominant world force in film production. Television ownership in the United States was beginning to take off, and box office receipts were starting to fall. In addition the House Committee for Un-American Activities was investigating Hollywood for the slightest trace of communist sympathies, driving the cream of its creative talent underground and causing the studios to operate the notorious blacklist. There were many in Hollywood who tried to hang on to the old way of life. Studios like MGM made interminable delays in hiving off their cinemas, and turned out anti-communist propaganda films. But the writing was on the wall. The days of the big studio with its mass production line and its permanently employed and highly paid staff were over. The only way forward was for Hollywood to close down or cut back its studios with their massive overheads. By reducing the flow of films to cinemas in a period of market decline, the majors ensured that the independent cinemas became even more dependent on their flow of films and, in turn, the distributors were able to take their own risks in financing the films they distributed. In these changed circumstances the Eady Levy offered Hollywood financial inducements to tread a path which it was likely to have taken anyway. Furthermore, American tax legislation encouraged investment overseas by American companies. During the 1950s therefore, Hollywood saw the growth of what came to be known as 'runaway production', whereby the major American film companies made their films outside Hollywood. The main beneficiaries of this development were Great Britain and Italy. The main losers were the Hollywood film workers whose colleagues in Great Britain and Italy benefited at their expense.

Large numbers of British films began to look more and more like Hollywood productions. Two early examples were Warner Brothers' *Captain Horatio Hornblower* (Raoul Walsh, 1951), starring Gregory Peck and Virginia Mayo, and *The African Queen* (John Huston, 1951) produced by Sam Spiegel for United Artists, starring Humphrey Bogart and Katherine Hepburn. Admittedly in both cases the scripts came from novels by the British author C.S.Forester, but they were both virtually indistinguishable from a Hollywood product. Only in a very marginal sense could the fact that they were British be discerned on the screen, from the choice of supporting actors and actresses or that of locations. The beneficiaries of these films were the British studios where they were shot and the British technicians who worked on them. Not surprisingly therefore, the Americans made no objection when the Eady Levy scheme was made statutory in 1957.

Not all films produced in Britain were Hollywood imitations however. At Ealing, Michael Balcon and his creative elite still produced films with a view of Britain and the British character dominated by consensus politics, and the Rank Organization produced several films in which the British officer class refought the Second World War and conquered the Nazis without the apparent assistance of either the Russians or the Americans. Towards the end of the decade, however, British films with a

new sense of realism began to emerge, usually adapted from
novels by writers from a working-class background who had
benefited from the opportunities offered by the 1944 Education
Act. Films such as *Look Back in Anger, Room At the Top, The
Loneliness of the Long Distance Runner, Saturday Night and
Sunday Morning* and *A Taste of Honey* were made, sometimes
with the help of NFFC, sometimes not. Much of the acting and
directing talent for these films came from the theatre, particularly
the Royal Court Theatre in London. More visually oriented
contributions came from cameramen working in the television
advertising industry and from set and costume designers trained
at the Royal College of Art.

The Americans were not slow to seize on the new new talents
and to use them for their own purposes, making films which
reflected their view of a joyous, classless pop culture with
anarchic tastes and sexually liberated behaviour. The so-called
'swinging London' was born. The image of Britain and British
culture was one selected and chosen by the American companies
for world-wide consumption. James Bond, the Beatles MBE,
Mary Quant fashions and tourist London were all part of the
package. The production of British films was booming and by
1969 nearly £33 million was being spent on the labour costs of
British film; an average labour of about £4,500 per minute. It
was estimated by the NFFC that some 90 per cent of British
production was wholly or partly financed by American resources.

But the bubble was to burst, and for four reasons. First, many
of the films made in Britain were making substantial losses in the
world market. Second, President Johnson had abolished the
American tax allowances on overseas investment in order to
finance the Vietnam war. Third, a combination of the level of the
pound against the dollar and the level of British labour costs
against those in Hollywood meant that it was no longer
substantially cheaper to produce films at Pinewood or Borehamwood rather than in Hollywood. And fourth, the heads of
the American companies wanted a tighter creative control over
the films they were financing. Labour costs for British films fell
by nearly two thirds during the next four years to £12.6 million.

To be fair to the British authorities, they had tried to preserve
some degree of autonomy for British film producers as the
industry had slowly but inexorably been taken over by American

interests. They had quietly introduced into secondary legislation a requirement that any company which benefited from the Eady Levy should be 'centrally managed and controlled' from Great Britain. In practice this meant that the American companies kept production offices in London, with a senior line producer in charge. But it became a regular practice for draft scripts to be shuttled back and forth across the Atlantic before the production finance was approved, and the role of the production office was limited to secondary casting, the employment of technicians and the supervision of budgets and schedules. Facilities companies flourished, but the key creative decisions were still taken in Los Angeles or in New York. The decline of the interest of the major American companies in Great Britain as a production centre for their films coincided with Britain's entry into the European Economic Community in 1973. Before Britain could join, the Government had to fulfil two conditions. The first was to broaden the requirement for cinemas to show a given quota of British films to include any films made within the European Community. This was enacted in the European Communities Act of 1972, but in real terms it made little difference since by and large there were enough British films to meet quota requirements, and most British audiences showed no interest in seeing either subtitled or poorly dubbed films which were originally shot in French, German or Italian. The only area where it made a marginal difference was to those cinemas which showed soft porn sex films. Audience interest in these films was primarily visual. A naked body is the same whether it speaks French, German or English, and British films of this genre were gradually replaced by films from other EEC countries. When the shortage of British films for quota purposes did threaten to be a real problem for cinemas there was little the government could do to force them to show films they wouldn't have shown normally. When a Labour government was in power the number of breaches of quota legislation rose, but no prosecutions were pursued. Under the Conservative government, the quota requirement was initially halved from 30 per cent to 15 per cent, then suspended, and finally abolished completely. The other condition imposed by the Common Market authorities was that the 'central management and control' requirement which was necessary for a company to benefit from the Eady Levy should be removed. This undertaking was given when the United Kingdom signed the Accession Treaty, but it was not implemented until nearly ten years later in July 1982.

The pressure from the Common Market authorities for this opening up of the film markets of member states stemmed from a belief that an open market would encourage strong community-wide production and distribution groups which would be able to compete with the major American companies. It took several years for them to realize that such a strategy did nothing to assist these groups in penetrating the American market, which accounts for over half the world market, nor did it prevent the American companies from investing their money wherever it suited them best – in Hollywood, Great Britain or Italy. It was not possible to erect a common external tariff wall against the American companies, nor to impose a distributors' quota without infringing the rules of GATT. The strength of the American companies lay in their worldwide distribution arrangements with which no branch of the European film industry could hope to compete.

The third aspect of Eady legislation which the Common Market authorities had in their sights was the requirement that a substantial proportion of labour costs for a British film should be paid to British citizens. This, they argued, was an infringement of the provisions of the Rome Treaty guaranteeing free movement of labour. Yet similar provisions existed in France, Italy and West Germany, and so the major film-producing nations of the Community were all opposed to the demands of the eurocrats in Brussels. When film legislation was revised in 1980, however, the Tory government decided that all new legislation should be 'Community proof'. It therefore broadened the Eady Levy provisions to extend the labour cost requirements to citizens of any member state of the Community. It was left to the British trade unions to protect their members' interests by insisting unilaterally that any Community technician employed on a British film should not be employed on terms less favourable than his or her British colleagues.

With quota legislation gone, the Eady Levy requirements modified, and with American finance being invested in Hollywood, the only element of traditional British film legislation which remained was the National Film Finance Corporation.

Although a new managing director, Mamoun Hassan, had been appointed by the Labour government to support and encourage new British talent he had only modest success. The NFFC set out to 'make not only films that appeal to a popular audience, but also films that will feed ideas and invention'. There were few commercial partners for these aspirations; few of the projects it supported got off the ground, and the NFFC lost more money. The Conservative government was embarrassed, and following a hasty review of film policy because the current legislation was due to expire, it decided to end the requirement for the NFFC to pay interest to the Treasury for its capital and to allocate the Corporation £1.5 million per year from the Eady Levy. This financial restructuring, together with some sales of assets gave the Corporation a modest profit over the next three years. Since 1980 it has succeded in co-financing the following: Diversity Music's *Babylon* (Franco Rosso, 1980); Memorial Film's *Memoirs of a Survivor* (David Gladwell, 1980); Lake Film Productions' *Gregory's Girl* (Bill Forsyth, 1981); Goldcrest Film International's *An Unsuitable Job For a Woman* (Chris Petit, 1981); Film and General/EMI's *Britannia Hospital* (Lindsay Anderson, 1982); Umbrella-Greenpoint's *Loose Connections* (Richard Eyre, 1983); and a number of shorts. There have been stories that the Board of the NFFC has disagreed over which projects to support and many of those for which it has announced support, have failed to find finance elsewhere. Many of the films it has supported have achieved critical success, but to date only one, *Gregory's Girl*, has been a popular success.

In a recent White Paper, the government announced that it intends to privatize the NFFC. A number of private investors including Thorn-EMI, Rank and Channel Four will take it over. They will invest £1.1 million per year for a period of three years and in addition they are expected to raise £0.2 million per year from the exploitation of the rights to old NFFC films. As an inducement the Treasury is giving them £1.5 million a year for the next five years. It is not just that the private sector is taking over the NFFC, the government is giving it £1.5 million a year to do so.

Outright subsidy for the private sector was the philosophy of the other arm of the Tory government's strategy for the film industry. In 1979 it ruled that investment in film production could be deemed as 'plant' for income tax purposes. This meant that companies trading profitably in other sectors such as banks, finance houses and various manufacturing groups, instead of paying corporation tax to help finance the defence, social services or education budgets would be able to invest their profits in film production and to thus write off these profits for tax purposes. The scheme was a licence to ensure that no company ever paid any tax, and in no time at all, the City of London had devised innumerable schemes to siphon off excess profits into film investment. Even though film financing was a risky form of investment, it was not as risky as handing your profits over to the tax authorities.

In the way in which it was initially formulated, the Government's ruling did not distinguish between British and foreign films and so naturally investors tried to co-finance films with the major American companies. One film financed in this way, ironically enough, was Paramount's *Reds* scripted by Trevor Griffiths and directed by Warren Beatty. In the 1982 budget, therefore, these tax concessions were restricted to British films. Investment in foreign films was clearly not permissible for tax purposes whereas investment in British films was. By the 1984 budget, however, the chancellor of the Exchequer had decided that the whole basis of capital allowances against tax relief was a nonsense and should be changed. Capital allowances were phased out and the special concessions available to the film industry went with it.

The concept of protection for the British film industry started out as the scheme of Imperial preference between the two World Wars. During the period between 1938 and 1972 arrangements were developed which encouraged the major American companies to invest in the production of British films, which in turn brought about the emergence of the infrastructure necessary for a national industry, such as film studios and laboratories and a highly skilled labour force of both technicians and performers. Since 1972, the entry of the United Kingdon into the Common Market has led to the reduction of the protective barriers of quota and Eady which ensured that at least some British films were shown in cinemas and that a substantial proportion of people employed in the making of British films were indeed British.

The realization that for the film industry to exist at all it is necessary for film production to be an attractive investment for British-based finance capital, has led to two schemes – first that of capital allowances for tax purposes, and now that of offering the private sector an inducement of £1.5 million per year to co-finance films in a privatized NFFC – both are designed to ensure that at least some private capital comes to British film production. It is argued that great opportunities exist for profitable investment in film production, and that may well be true. But in no case can it be argued that profitable investment either in films produced by British companies or in films crewed by British technicians are necessarily the same as investing in films which are the cultural expression of the British people.

The philosophy of protection for the British film industry was never wholly successful because it studiously ignored the content and the social impact of the films which the so-called British film industry produced. Today only a few tattered remnants of that policy remain. The debate on the future of film policy in the United Kingdom must necessarily concern itself not simply with the size and shape of the industry but also with the nature and quality of the films which it supports, and who is responsible for them.

8. Censorship

The traditional way in which the state has concerned itself with the nature and quality of films shown in cinemas has been through the mechanism of censorship. It was the local authorities who first expressed an interest in licensing cinemas in Great Britian because of the dangers to the public from the fire hazards associated with the early film stock which was nitrate based. The Cinematograph Act of 1909 made no mention of censorship. Its purpose was 'to make better provisions for securing safety at cinematographic and other exhibitions'. However, the London County Council used the new Act to require cinemas to remain closed on Sundays, and when the Bermondsey Bioscope Company appealed against the ruling on the grounds that such a condition was beyond the scope of the Act, they were told in the High Court by the Lord Chief Justice that local authorities could impose whatever conditions they chose so long as they were not unreasonable. It was this decision which opened the way to the present system of film censorship, in which local authorities have the power to say which films can be shown in a cinema.

For the film trade, the possibility of various local authorities taking different decisions about the suitability of the same film, posed a very real threat to the screening of a film throughout the country. What the trade wanted was a situation where the same film could be shown in all cinemas without interference from local authorities or their watch committees. A similar situation was to arise in the US a decade later when it became clear that film censorship was a matter for individual state legislation, whereas the industry wanted films to be shown in the same version throughout the whole of the US. The solution proposed in both cases was the same, a self censorship system operated by the film industry itself. In the United Kingdom the censoring body was to be the British Board of Film Censors (BBFC) which was set up in 1913. In the US it was to be the Production Code Administration of the Motion Picture Producers and Distributors Association of America, known colloquially as the Hays Office after its first president, Will H. Hays. A similar industry body for self censorship has been set up in the Federal Republic of Germany.

The parallel histories of the BBFC and the Hays Office reveal how a small group of men and women developed dictatorial control over the content of films shown in cinemas. In both cases they set out, not simply to ensure that the films were acceptable to the local authorities or to the state legislatures, but also to develop codes of practice which ensured that all films fell in with the ideological requirements of the dominant political and commercial pressure groups in each country. In Great Britain it was the influence of the establishment, the Conservative party and the susceptibilities of the Roman Catholic church which became dominant. In the US it was the influence of the Roman Catholic church and of big business which held sway.

The reason why censorship developed in this way, was not because the industry wanted to create a climate in which the creative abilities of individual directors and scriptwriters could flourish, but because the producers of the films and their financial backers wanted to be assured that their films would receive no interference from outside, once they had been completed. In order to achieve this aim, both censorship boards developed a system of vetting film scripts in advance of production and thus, effectively, a system of double censorship was established for films which were produced domestically. The scripts were censored before the films were made, and in many cases rejected outright. The films were then censored a second time, once they were completed, before the local authorities or the state legislatures had a chance to say whether or not they felt the censorship board was being too severe in its strictures. The system was not one designed to permit the greatest degree of creative freedom, it was one designed to ensure the highest degree of political, religious or commercial conformism.

In the United Kingdom the BBFC openly admitted that it would pass nothing that it felt would demoralize the public since it was convinced that 'a not inconsiderable proportion' of the public were people 'of immature judgement'. This 'immaturity' among cinema-goers was not confined simply to moral matters, it also extended to political issues. The main controversies over the banning or cutting of films between the two World Wars were political. In 1926 the BBFC consulted the Home Secretary, Sir William Joynson-Hicks, before banning the Russian film classic, *Battleship Potemkin* (Sergei Eisenstein, 1925) on the grounds that it might incite political revolution in Britain. It also banned another Russian classic, *The Mother* (Vsevolod Pudovkin, 1926). Two years later, it banned British Dominion Films' *Dawn* (Herbert Wilcox, 1928) which dealt with the life of the British nurse Edith Cavell, who was tried and executed for spying during the First World War by the German authorities in Belgium. This decision followed a private conversation between T.P. O'Connor, the President of the BBFC and the then Foreign Secretary, Sir Austen Chamberlain who had been delegated to talk to him by the Cabinet, who feared that the showing of the film might upset Anglo-German relations. Another film banned during this period was the three-minute short film *The Peace of Britain* (edited and co-scripted by the socialist film-maker Paul Rotha, 1936) which opposed spending public money on re-armament and argued instead that Britain should back the League of Nations as an international peace-keeper. Fortunately this last ban was rescinded following protests in the national press.

The BBFC also banned films which might upset religious groups or royalty. *Martin Luther* was banned in 1929 since it was felt that it might upset Roman Catholics, and it was probably not a matter of pure chance that both T.P. O'Connor, the President of the Board until 1929, and indeed his successor but one, Lord Tyrrell, were both Catholics. The Board also banned any reference to the then Prince of Wales in films and what it termed 'libellous' reflections on royal dynasties. Its ban went further than that, however. All depictions of Queen Victoria, whether libellous or not, were banned until 1937, 100 years after her accession to the throne. Even then, the only representations of the old Queen that were permitted were those that received official approval. Herbert Wilcox's film *Victoria the Great* made in 1937 received the official endorsement of Edward VIII and his next film, *Sixty Glorious Years*, was not only cleared by the

Palace, but partly scripted by Sir Robert Vansittart of the foreign office. These officially sanctioned hagiographies were passed by the BBFC without comment, even though they were later shown to have been historically innaccurate. However, a proposal for a film which was submitted to the BBFC in the same year about the relationship between the Queen and John Brown, entitled *John Brown, Servant of the Queen*, was turned down as being 'quite unfit for exhibition in this country'.

Next in line for the censor's disapproval were any films which held up to contempt, or called into question, the behaviour of members of the British armed forces. In particular, films dealing with India were not permitted to show British officers behaving in a reprehensible manner, nor were they able to suggest that the Native States might be 'disloyal' to the Crown. The controls over the ways in which the armed forces, and in particular the British officer class, were portrayed had, of course, both political and professional implications. The portrayal of doctors, however, was not a political question, it was a professional and social question. Here too the BBFC moved to protect the image of the middle classes. Nine proposals for films were banned between 1934 and 1937 because they threatened the image of the medical profession, including a film of George Bernard Shaw's *The Doctor's Dilemma*. The religious profession was also protected by the BBFC, and a further four proposals were banned during the same period because of the ways in which the priests in the films behaved.

The BBFC was not only concerned with the ways in which the middle class professions – the church, the army and the law – were portrayed, it was also concerned to control the way in which the working class was portrayed – or, more precisely, was allowed to see itself. The Board had a very clear view on the way in which the relations between labour and capital were to be depicted. 'Strikes or labour unrest', wrote Colonel J. C. Hanna, the senior examiner of film scripts, 'where the scene is laid in England (sic) have never been shown in any detail. It is impossible to show such strikes without taking a definite side either with or against the strikers and this would at once range the film as political propaganda of a type that we have always held to be unsuitable for exhibition in this country'. Predictably, the dominant image of the working class during the 1930s was a docile one, reflecting the establishment's view of Britain rather than that of the working class. When industrial conflict was shown, it was from a capitalist perspective as in Gaumont British's *Red Ensign* (Michael Powell, 1934) – retitled *Strike* in the USA – which showed how the managing director of a Clydeside shipbuilding company risks everything, including his own money, to build a new ship and overcomes sabotage and strikes on the way. When the working class was the central feature of a film, the films were anodyne vehicles featuring music hall stars such as George Formby or Gracie Fields. Even here, films which had a dash of social comment such as the Gracie Fields vehicle, ATP's *Sing As We Go* (Basil Dean, 1934), which was scripted by J.B. Priestley, were emasculated during production and the hard-nosed social comment removed. The major scandal during the 1930s was the censor's consistent refusal to allow the filming of Walter Greenwood's classic novel, *Love on the Dole*. During the Second World War, however, when it was, necessary to convince the British people that they were fighting the war to defend liberty and to build a better Britain, it was filmed, at the insistence of Sir Kenneth Clark who was responsible for propaganda at the Ministry of Information.

The BBFC also set out to regulate the way in which the British people saw the world beyond its shores. The relationship between Great Britain and foreign countries was a matter of ongoing concern for the BBFC. It was their justification for banning *Dawn* in 1928. There were numerous examples of interference in the ways in which foreign countries were depicted in films during the 1930s, but perhaps the most important, was the consistent refusal of the BBFC to allow any criticism of Nazi Germany to appear in films between 1933 and the start of the Second World War on the grounds that it might offend the Nazi authorities. In 1938, they banned Time Inc.'s 'March of Time' film *Inside Nazi Germany*; and as late as 1938 they refused the Boulting Brothers permission to make *Pastor Hall* a film about the life of Pastor Martin Niemoller who was persecuted by the Nazis. Three months later, however, when war was declared, it was rushed into production. The only way open to film-makers who opposed Nazi activities for getting around this ban was either to use historical analogy as was the case in the Gaumont British film *Jew Süss*, produced in 1934, which was about anti-semitism in 18th century Würtemburg, or to outwit the censors by implying spies were Nazis by portraying them as mid-Europeans with guttural accents, as was the case in three of the Hitchcock films made for Gaumont British – *The Thirty-Nine Steps* (1935), *The Secret Agent* (1936), and *Sabotage* (1936).

In the United Kingdom the BBFC was much more closely influenced by the political establishment than by the film trade. In the US, however, the Hays Office mediated much more directly between the industry and the pressure groups, particularly those led by the Roman Catholic church such as the Legion of Decency. As a result, the Hays Office developed a much more sophisticated notion of censorship than the BBFC. Naturally both bodies had their bans on nudity, on swearing and on immoral behaviour, but when it came to the representation of the real world and the institutions within it, the Hays Office could be quite sophisticated. Part of the reason for this was its willingness to enter into the intricacies of film production in order to achieve its ends and to try and square the circle of reconciling a degree of artistic freedom with external commercial, political and religious pressures. Another factor was the strong resistance, within the American polity, to curbs on free speech.

In the beginning the Hays Office was just as draconian as the BBFC and just as reluctant to stand up for the right of film-makers. At the request of the Yellow Cab Company it made sure that yellow cabs were never involved in cops and robber chases, so that the Yellow Cab Company need have no fear of losing business as a result of the way in which their cabs were used in films. Similarly, it banned scenes showing pool rooms as low-class dives in order to appease the National Billiards Association, and it banned scenes showing smoking in bed in order to appease the American Hotel Association. Scenes showing canned beer were also eliminated from films in order to appease the Glass Blowers Association.

It soon became clear to the Hays Office, however, that to go on banning scenes in this simple-minded way could actually lead to such anodyne and schmaltzy films that audiences would stay away. It learnt to admit that there were both good and bad things in the world. The important thing was for the dramatic structure of the narrative to show that the good always triumphed over the bad, and that although one member of a trade or profession might be immoral or a criminal, there were always others, and normally several others, who were honest and upright. It took special care to regulate the portrayals of lawyers, judges and courtroom scenes during the late 1930s at a time when it was becoming increasingly recognized that many lawyers and judges were in the pay of corrupt city bosses, and that there were frequently close links between organized crime and members of the legal profession. It had to balance these facts against the pressures from the authorities and from the legal professions themselves to show lawyers and judges as totally incorruptible, and it was prepared to produce detailed statistical analyses to show that good triumphed over bad in Hollywood films.

This balancing of good and evil, of moral and immoral behaviour, led to the Hays Office developing a thesis of 'compensating moral values' which permitted a fictional character in a film to commit a crime or to behave immorally, provided that it was shown in another scene in the film either that the particular act concerned was committed under duress, or unknowingly, or that the character repented of that act later in the film, or realized that it brought her or him consequent personal unhappiness. The close links between the Roman Catholic church and the Hays Office ensured that it was Catholic morality that was the basis of the moral order in Hollywood films.

The advent of the Second World War and the arrival of television meant that the cinema ceased to be the dominant mass medium of the people. In the United Kingdom and United States the criteria for film censorship were eased as cinemas came under greater commercial pressure to hang on to their audiences. In the United Kingdom the BBFC acquired a new secretary in 1958, John Trevelyan. With the support of the film trade, the BBFC ceased to be dominated by a president who was effectively appointed by the Home Secretary and in turn was run by a team of a president and a secretary. The president was appointed on a consultancy basis with a general responsibility for policy, but it was the secretary who became the chief executive. The net result of this was that political intervention in censorship decisions declined and the criteria for censorship requirements centred principally on questions of artistic taste and their relation to representations of nudity, sexual behaviour and obscenity. Certain scenes which showed 'how to' commit various criminal offences from making petrol bombs to taking drugs or stealing cars were also removed to prevent them being imitated by members of the public.

In the US the Hays Office lost its control over the content of films for a number of reasons. As in the United Kingdom, the mass family audience switched from the cinema to television causing a drop in attendances. As a result more foreign films began to be shown in American cinemas bringing different cultural and artistic values to American screens. Finally, the anti-trust judgement of the US Supreme Court which ruled that Hollywood divorce its exhibition interests from its production and distribution interests, meant that Hollywood was no longer the closed cartel that it was prior to the Second World War. For economic reasons, the value of the Hays Office to the industry was increasingly questioned. The courts too were questioning the legality of the Hays office. Although the Supreme Court had originally decided in 1915 that individual states had the power to censor films, Mr Justice Douglas wrote in the Supreme Court's ruling in the Paramount anti-trust case, that the court had 'no doubt that moving pictures, like newspapers and radio, are included in the press whose freedom is guaranteed by the First Amendment'.

Four years later, as a result of pressure from Cardinal Spellman and the Catholic church, the New York censors banned as 'sacrilegious' the Italian film *The Miracle* (Roberto Rossellini, 1948) even though they had already permitted it to play in a New York art cinema for two months. The Supreme Court ruled that censorship of a film as sacrilegious was not permitted as it would favour one religion over another. Although *The Miracle* decision was a blow against official censorship it was the decision of United Artists to release two films produced by Otto Preminger, *The Moon Is Blue* (1953) and *The Man With The Golden Arm* (1956) without the approval of the Hays Office that was the breakthrough within the industry. The Hays Office had refused to pass the former film because it dealt with adultery and had rejected the latter because it dealt with drug-taking. Both films were commercially successful and it was clear that commercially successful films could be produced without being submitted for censorship.

The decline of the Hays Office led to the resurgence of a number of citizens' pressure groups and to the increased activity of state and city censorship boards, particularaly those in New York, Maryland, Ohio and Chicago. As in the United Kingdom, the censors were concerned almost exclusively with questions of nudity and sex. The censorship boards imposed decisions which were based on personal prejudices, impulses and reactions of individual censors. In Chicago, where the censorship board was administered by the police department, it was composed entirely of the widows of policemen. The censorship overseer boasted, 'The courts don't lay down any guidelines for us.'

Since the Supreme Court had ruled in *The Miracle* decision in 1952 that films were protected by the First Amendment, the struggles between the film trade and the local censorship boards were centred on the question of whether a film could be defined as 'obscene' or not. The censorship boards tried to categorize everything that they objected to as 'obscene' and it was another five years before the Supreme Court, in a case concerning the John Cleland novel, *Memoirs of a Woman of Pleasure*, required that the work in question should lack *all* redeeming social value.

This 'narrow' definition of the word severely restricted the activities of local censorship boards, and for a number of reasons, film producers preferred the new situation. Firstly, the burden of proof of obscenity was on the prosecution and secondly the 'narrow' definition of obscenity meant that the probability of a successful prosecution was quite low. Thirdly, most films did not need to be submitted for censorship, and fourthly many films were exhibited at cinemas and continued to run during the decision of an obscenity case, since many courts had ruled that a film could not be seized until a preliminary hearing had been held.

As a result of the change in the balance of power between the film trade and the local authorities, some local authorities tried extra-legal tactics in order to try and prevent films being shown. Arrests and confiscations were used as techniques for harassment, and cinema exhibitors were accused of running 'disorderly houses' making it necessary for these exhibitors to go to court to take out injunctions against the local authorities. A city council in a Los Angeles suburb held up approval for the construction of a cinema complex until it received an assurance that no X-rated films would be shown there; a Florida city authority shut off the electricity and water a few minutes before *Fanny Hill Meets Lady Chatterley* (Barry Mahon, George Matsui, 1967) was to be shown there, invoked a technicality to revoke the cinema's licence and then refused to issue a new one; and in a Boston suburb uniformed policemen were sent to a cinema showing *Bullit* (Peter Yates, 1968) to turn back all children under 16 coming to see it. The exhibitor was then told that he would have to pay the policemen's wages.

In Dallas, Texas, a board was set up in 1965 to determine which films were 'not suitable for young persons' and persons under 16 were forbidden to see them. One film which the Board decided was unsuitable was United Artists' *Viva Maria* (Louis Malle, 1965) starring Brigitte Bardot, Jeanne Moreau and George Hamilton. The exhibitor, Interstate Circuit, fought the decision and the Supreme Court ruled against the Dallas board on the grounds that the Dallas law did not require the board to give its reasons for its decisions. Although a triumph had been scored against censorship, a victory had not been won against classification of films, for the Court ruled that its decision did not preclude a more carefully drafted classification scheme.

Shortly after, however, New York won a case in which the Supreme Court ruled it legal to ban pornographic books, and California considered a bill for classifying films. The victory in the *Viva Maria* case was a pyrrhic one, and during the next five months there were frantic attempts between the Motion Picture Association of America (MPAA) which represented the major film companies, the National Association of Theatre Owners (NATO) which represented the cinema owners and the International Film Importers and Distributors of America (IFIDA) which was responsible for distributing foreign films, to agree a classification scheme for films which would be acceptable to all sections of the trade and which would forestall legislative classification by a host of different cities and states. In October 1968 the industry's classification scheme was officially announced. It would apply to all films released in the US from the following month. There would be four ratings: G (general) open to all; M (mature) recommended for mature audiences: R (Restricted) to which under 16s had to be accompanied by a parent; and X banned to all audiences under 16. This scheme apart from a couple of minor modifications – the M classification has become PG (Parental Guidance) and the 16 year limit has been raised to 17 – is still in force today.

Within the United Kingdom, the practice of film classification has existed as an adjunct to film censorship since the 1920s. From 1922 until 1953 the A classification required a child under the age of 16 to be accompanied by a parent or guardian. In January 1951 the Board introduced the X certificate for films designated for adults only, and 20 years later a new system was introduced which was similar, although not identical to, the MPAA classification scheme. The U certificate remained, the A certificate was for films which anybody could see, but which contained adult material similar to the R-rating (later PG) in the USA. A new category, AA, was for films for which audiences had to be at least 14 years old, while the audiences for X certificate films had to be at least 18 years old. The extra classification permitted the Board to distinguish between films which were not suitable for children in that their themes dealt in part with some aspect of sex, and films which dealt wholly or explicitly with sex and which were clearly aimed only at adult audiences.

Although there was a growing similarity between the MPAA rating system and the BBFC classification system, the crucial difference that remained was that the MPAA did not pre-censor films for adult audiences whereas the BBFC did. The UK, unlike the US, has no written constitution and certainly no 'first amendment' to protect the freedom of speech or of the press. For the British authorities, the capacity of the BBFC to decide whether or not a film was obscene, was a way of ensuring that the public was given little say in deciding public standards of obscenity. The Director of Public Prosecutions (DPP) was happy to leave these questions to the BBFC because, as he told the House of Commons Committee on Obscene Publications in 1956, he would be unlikely to prosecute a film for obscenity since he would also 'have to put the British Board of Film Censors in the dock because they have aided and abetted in the commission of that particular offence'. It was not surprising therefore that when the new Obscene Publications Act was passed in 1959 it did not apply to films since the existence of the

BBFC was thought to render it unnecessary. The cosy alliance between the DPP and the BBFC has continued to this day, and there has been no occasion since that time when the DPP has given serious consideration to prosecuting a film which has been given a certificate by the BBFC.

This alliance was implicitly challenged, however, by the Greater London Council which had a more relaxed approach to censorship than the BBFC. It permitted several films to be exhibited in the Greater London area which had not received a certificate from the BBFC, including one called *More About the Language of Love*. Although films were not covered by the Obscene Publications Act, they were covered by the common law of indecency, a less serious offence in the eyes of the law than that of obscenity. Under pressure from Raymond Blackburn MP, the DPP took action against *More About the Language of Love* which was found to be indecent. Meanwhile the Law Commission had been reviewing the criminal law and had proposed that all the common law provisions relating to public morals and decency, including those which had been hastily summoned to prevent the cinema exhibition of *More About the Language of Love* should be abolished as old-fashioned and anachronistic. If this proposal had been implemented however, it would have meant that there would be nothing to prevent individual local authorities, such as the GLC, from giving a licence for the exhibition of any film they chose, and which the DPP would have no legal means to prohibit. Furthermore, many cinemas were technically cinema clubs and could therefore show uncensored films. Accordingly, films were brought within the provision of the Obscene Publications Act by the Criminal Law Act of 1977, whether they were shown in cinemas or not.

There are a number of other areas of the law, apart from the Obscene Publications Act which also regulate the content of films. These include the Cinematograph Films (Animals) Act and the Protection of Children Act. The former prevents films which involve cruelty to animals, and the latter prevents films which involve the sexual degradation of children. But it was obscenity which continued to be the recurring obsession of the public and the authorities. The government set up a new committee in 1977, chaired by Professor Bernard Williams, to enquire into obscenity and film censorship.

Despite taking a fairly relaxed view about obscenity in general, the Williams Committee rejected the view that while the classification system of the BBFC served a valuable function, the cinema should have parallel treatment to the theatre. That was to say there should be no pre-censorship of films shown to adults, as was the case in the US and that the distributor or exhibitor accused of showing an obscene film should be able to defend it in the courts. The Committee disagreed. 'Film,' it argued, 'is a uniquely powerful instrument: the close-up, fast cutting, the sophistication of modern make-up and special effects techniques, the heightening effects of sound effects and music, all combine on the large screen to produce an impact which no other medium can create.'

This view stemmed from seeing a reel of excerpts from banned films which were shown to the Committee by the BBFC as part of its evidence which consisted almost exclusively of highly explicit depictions of mutilation, savagery, menace and humiliation that appeared to emphasize the pleasures of sadism. Although, as the Committee admitted, it may be that such graphically presented sadistic material served only as a vivid object of fantasy and did no harm at all, there was certainly no conclusive evidence to show that this was its only result, and that for these reasons caution was a better strategy than freedom. Accordingly, the Committee departed from the predominantly liberal policy of the remainder of its report and recommended that the licensing of cinemas for censorship purposes be taken away from local authorities, and that the BBFC be reconstituted as a state censorship body with an established appeal procedure. In addition it recommended a change in the classification system, raising the age limit for the AA certificate to 16 years and the introduction of a new '18R' certificate for restricted exhibition of X films in an uncut version.

The main recommendations of the Williams Committee were not taken up, but some changes were made in the classification system. The age limit for the AA classification was raised by one year and it was now called '15'; the 'A' classification was retitled 'PG', the same as in the MPAA rating; and a new classification was introduced '18R' for more sexually explicit films. Although the Williams Committee proposal to convert the BBFC into a statutory body was not taken up, the BBFC was to become, at least in part, a statutory body as a result of the Video Recordings Act of 1984. Whereas it had been possible to control the showing of films by licensing cinemas and, since 1982, cinema clubs, the advent of videocassette recording meant that it was no longer possible to control film content by licensing the premises on which they were to be shown. As a result of pressures from various groups, the Home Office rejected the proposal of the British Videogram Association for a voluntary self-censorship scheme along the lines of the BBFC and insisted that the censorship of videocassettes was to be the responsibility of a body appointed by the state even though, according to a public opinion poll commissioned by the British Videogram Asociation, 65 per cent of the public felt that the government should not be involved in matters of censorship.

One of the main reasons for this switch in policy was an astute campaign which was conducted by supporters of state censorship led by Mary Whitehouse. An *ad hoc* lobby of churchmen, MPs and academics, calling itself the Parliamentary Group Video Enquiry, produced a report entitled 'Video violence and children' which claimed that nearly four children in ten watched video 'nasties' and that six year olds were 'hooked on horror, sex and violence'. A few months later the final version of the report claimed that 45 per cent of youngsters between 7 and 16 had watched a video 'nasty' and that for boys alone, the figure was more than one half.

The first version of the report was released just before the Video Recordings Bill had its second reading in the House of Commons, and the second version a few months later when it went before the House of Lords. In between the two versions, the Roman Catholic and Methodist representatives on the group's sponsoring committee had withdrawn their support, and researchers at Oxford Polytechnic's Television Research Unit, which had processed the results, dissociated themselves from the report claiming that the project director, Dr Clifford Hill, had misused the data which they had processed. More seriously, an attempt was made by two applied psychologists at Aston University to repeat the enquiry carried out by the Parliamentary Video Group. They obtained copies of the questionnaires used in the enquiry which they felt was far too complex for six-year-old children. They hypothesized that children, instead of ringing the videos that they had seen as asked, would simply ring those videos they had heard of. Accordingly, Dr Guy Cumberbatch and Dr Paul Bates made some subtle alterations by changing some of the video titles to purely fictitious ones such as *Zombies from Beyond Space*. Of the children who claimed to have seen video 'nasties', 82 per cent claimed to have seen videos which did not exist! So much for the validity of the Parliamentary Video Group's research methods.

The second tactic adopted by the Parliamentary Video Group was to arrange for the screening of a 20-minute videotape of the worst excerpts from 'video nasties', first in the House of Commons, and later in the House of Lords, on the eve of the reading of the Video Recordings Bill. Not surprisingly MPs and peers both came away reeling from an overdose of the worst excesses of the videocassettes available to the public and duly supported the passage of the Video Recordings Bill through Parliament. There is nothing like a short sharp dose of horrifying extracts to persuade legislators of the need for pre-censorship as the British Board of Film Censors had proved when it met the Williams Committee six years earlier.

Having acceded to the demands for the state censorship of videocassettes, the legislators failed to address themselves to the really serious questions which surrounded the cultural, social and political accountability of the new censorship body which the Home Secretary was authorized to designate for the purpose. Although the ostensible purpose of the Bill was to outlaw sex and violence, the Act does not limit the pre-censorship of videocassettes to these areas. Although the government has denied that it would use the Act to censor films for reasons of politics as well as on grounds of decency, it refused an amendment which would have limited the Act to these areas and, perhaps more ominously, it is keeping secret the guidelines which it is laying down for the British Board of Film Censors. We now have on the statute book an Act which permits the pre-censorship of videocassettes for political purposes.

Another problem concerns the comparative standards which are to be adopted by the BBFC in classifying films destined for cinema release and films destined as videocassettes. In the US, the Federal Republic of Germany and Australia, the criteria used for both markets are the same. In the United Kingdom, however, the Video Recordings Act requires that the classification certificates for videocassettes must have special regard for the fact that videocassettes will be viewed in the home, a phrase which is meant to imply a more stringent system of classification than that allowed in cinemas. This is liable to cause a number of difficulties, with different versions of the same film being shown in cinemas and on videocassette, causing problems of recutting for the distributors and problems for the consumer of knowing what he or she is buying or renting. No longer will the person who buys or rents a videocassette know whether it is the same film that was reviewed by the film critics when they saw it in the cinema.

It is possible to foresee that the Video Recordings Act will raise far more problems than it solves. All videocassettes, with only minor exceptions, will have to be pre-censored and the BBFC is currently proposing a charge of £4.00 per minute, or £720 for a 3-hour videocassette, even if no censor alterations are required. This will be a major disincentive for the small distributor. The BBFC will become a hybrid body, accountable to two masters, the Home Office and the film trade, and the long-term rationalization of this situation may well be to bring censorship of cinema films in line with that for videocassettes. We now have a state censorship body for cinema films which will censor films according to secret guidelines laid down by the Home Secretary – a truly Orwellian enactment for 1984! In these circumstances it may prove to be very important that there is not yet any requirement to pre-censor 16 millimetre films which are shown to film societies and colleges and which are not shown in licensed cinemas.

Although it is censorship by public or semi-public bodies such as the BBFC, the Director of Public Prosecutions and local licensing authorities which normally attract attention, censorship can also be exercised by private individuals and interest groups, before a film goes into production. This occurs in three main ways: through the use of the libel laws; through the provision of filming facilities and through the provision of production finance. In a famous court case brought by Princess Youssopoff, the daughter of the Czar who was overthrown by the Russians in 1917, it was decided that the portrayal of a living person in a fiction film could constitute libel. Princess Youssopoff claimed that MGM's *Rasputin* (Richard Boleslavsky, 1933) implied that she had been raped by Rasputin and was therefore unchaste. This, she claimed, was historically untrue and 'tended to lower the opinion which right-thinking members of society would have of her'. The courts found in her favour and MGM was fined £25,000 for libelling her.

As a result of this decision, the film distributors and the banks who finance the production of films now take great care before a film goes into production to ensure that they have written approval of the script and treatment of any living individual who is shown in the film. The effect of this has been to grant individuals who are portrayed in the film effective pre-production censorship over this matter. That power can extend not only to the way in which they themselves are portrayed, but also to the way in which the film portrays their friends or members of their family, such as their parents or a spouse, who may no longer be alive. Films which purport to reconstruct recent historical events must therefore always be open to the charge that what they show is hagiography rather than history.

One area of film production where this has played an important role is in films which reconstruct episodes of military history such as those based on the Second World War. Films which contain the portrayal of someone who is still alive, even if it is only the spouse or the child of a former member of the armed forces, will have been approved by that person in advance. Given that it is normally the politicians and the senior officers who feature in the films as individuals, and the lower ranks usually feature as anonymous individuals or as an unidentifiable part of the masses, it is the establishment or their relatives, who are able to censor the film-maker's portrayals of the past, and therefore, to some extent at least, control how they are represented in history. Ordinary people are not identified as individuals and therefore have no such power.

The private censorship of films at a pre-production stage can also be exercised by those who are asked to help with providing facilities for the making of the film. The most obvious examples are when a film-maker needs to use facilities which cannot be satisfactorily reproduced in the film studio. If, for instance, a film-maker wants to recreate a battle scene, he or she may well approach a government department for assistance with the provision of say, battleships or fighter aircraft. Access to these facilities may well be dependent on the prior approval of the script by the government department concerned. This prior veto can also be exercised by industrialists. When the film-makers, financed by the drama department of West Deutscher Rundfunk (the Cologne television station) were trying to make a trilogy of films which portrayed the struggles between labour and capital in the engineering industry, the industrialists refused them access to any of the factories that they wanted to use. In the end WDR had to apply political pressure to obtain the use of a state-owned factory for filming.

This subtle but effective form of pre-production censorship was used in the United Kingdom during the Second World War by the Ministry of Information. Initially the MOI had wanted to finance its own feature films, but it was only able to co-finance one, *The Forty-ninth Parallel* (Michael Powell and Emeric Pressburger, 1940). After an enquiry by the Select Committee on National Expenditure, it was decided that the MOI should not continue to participate in financing feature films because it was financially too risky and because the intended propaganda message was likely to be out of date before the production of the film was completed.

The MOI therefore developed a new strategy in its attempt to exert the maximum control on the ideology of British films being made commercially. It was able to do this in two ways. For any film which needed to use military facilities, these would only be made available if the MOI approved the script and its ideological message. A second, but more wide-ranging mechanism for control, was the power of the MOI to determine which actors, scriptwriters, directors and technicians were released from military duties to make films. Under the war regulations, every able-bodied man and most able-bodied women were called up, and it was only with the authorizations of the MOI that key film stars such as David Niven, Laurence Olivier and Michael Redgrave could be released from military activities to appear in commercially produced films. This power over the selection of film stars and technicians ceased once the war was over, but the power of a government department to control the content of a film which wishes to use governmental facilities still remains today.

Perhaps the most subtle form of pre-production censorship is the power of censorship wielded by the sources of production finance for a film. Not unnaturally, the company or organization which is financing the production of the film will wish to ensure that the film makes a profit. The person responsible for taking the decision will therefore wish to take into account a whole range of factors and opinions before deciding to go ahead, and many of these will, in effect, constitute a form of pre-production censorship.

When a major Hollywood company is financing a feature film for international release, it will normally require the film-maker to obtain a certificate from the film censors. This requirement may not simply be for the film to be censored, it may specify that the film must obtain a specific censorship certificate, such as PG or an R rating in the US or a PG or '15' certificate in the United Kingdom, in order to ensure that the film can reach its maximum audience. The finance source will also, as shown earlier, wish to ensure that it is not vulnerable to a libel suit if the film represents on the screen anyone who is still alive. Beyond these formal requirements the banks, often the ultimate source of film finance, have sought to exert control over the content of films in a number of subtle ways. The details of these attempts have varied over the years, but they are always subtle, often denied and frequently difficult to document. In 1933 'Doc' Attilio Henry Giannini, a senior executive of the Bank of Italy, later to become the Bank of America, and brother of its founder Amadeo Peter Giannini, told the West Coast Association of Hollywood producers that if they wanted the bank to continue financing film production, it might become 'a matter of conscience' unless Hollywood was prepared to allow the Hays Office to censor films on a mandatory basis. Here was a clear example of the major film bank of Hollywood using financial pressure to persuade film-makers to accede to the pressures of the Roman Catholic church for compulsory censorship of all films by the Hays Office.

Times have changed since 1933, however, and the banks have become more subtle in their methods. 'Doc' Giannini went on to become one of the members of the voting trusts which controlled Universal Pictures and Columbia Pictures, and for a short while became president of United Artists. His stint as president of United Artists was short lived but the strategy of controlling film production at arm's length through cross-directorships is one which continues to this day. In a survey of the six major Hollywood film companies which was carried out in 1978, it was shown that between 11 and 67 per cent of the Board directors were associated with major banks and that, on average, the banks held nearly 40 per cent of the directorships of the Hollywood corporations. Today the banks 'look to the company' to decide which films to make and to ensure that they are both profitable and ideologically acceptable. It is the Boards of Directors who appoint the senior company executives who are expected to reconcile these aims, and it is the banks who exert a key influence in deciding who is appointed. Outside the big umbrella provided by the Hollywood majors, the independent film producer will normally have to try and finance a film with money raised from a number of different sources, each acquiring a different part of the film copyright. Some investors will acquire the distribution rights for a particular country or group of countries, others may acquire the distribution rights for a particular medium, such as cable television, videocassette or broadcast television. Clearly, for any one film project there are a multitude of possibilities for co-financing. Each potential partner will have his own particular preferences and objections and a film project may have to be redrafted and reshaped, rescripted and recast in order to put together a project which is ultimately acceptable to all partners. Along the way, many aspects of the original project may be dropped and new emphases added. It is almost impossible to determine where censorship ends and where creativity begins.

It is impossible to raise the finance for a major film without taking into account what is going to happen to the film in the US, which constitutes some 55 per cent of the world cinema market. This means that no major cinema film is likely to be made which its financiers do not consider will do well in the US. It is the tastes of the American market which dominate world film production for all large budget films. The only films which can ignore the American market are those which can recoup their costs in more limited markets, such as national or regional markets, with or without the help of television finance and a television release.

Film censorship and film finance are inextricably linked. The censors can only censor those films which someone has chosen to finance. The financiers on the other hand only produce those films which they judge will meet the approval of the censors. The censors and the financiers try to anticipate both what the marketplace wants and the extent to which they can impose their world view on the public. It is common to represent the censor as the hard face of the authoritarian state stifling the creative activity of the film-maker. It is equally common to represent the film-maker as struggling to give the public the films it wants to see. In truth, both the state and the film financiers exert their censorships in different ways.

9. Patronage

The form of aid which the state can give to film has convention-
ally been classified as 'automatic' or 'selective' aid. Automatic
aid refers to financial support which is given to a film which
fulfils certain criteria regardless of its content. Selective aid
refers to financial support which is given to a film and which
depends either on the content of the film itself, or upon the
individual people who are making it. The major Western
European countries, such as Great Britain, France, Italy and
West Germany have traditionally used automatic aid schemes,
like Great Britain's Eady Levy arrangements, to support their
film industries, but both the regulations of the Common Market
and the increasing internationalization of the film industry have
come to mean that automatic aid schemes of this nature make
less and less sense in reality. The British government, which has
been the first to grasp this nettle, is proposing to abolish the
Eady Levy arrangements in its current White Paper on Film
Policy.

The second form of automatic aid scheme, although frequently
unremarked as such, is the preferential taxation arrangements
which are frequently permitted to investors in film production.
Until this year, the British government offered this form of aid,
and there are currently similar arrangements available to film
producers in a number of countries including the United States,
Australia, Canada, and Jamaica. Other countries also operate
schemes which grant preferential tax rates to film exhibitors or
film distributors. Tax relief schemes are popular with the film
industries and their pressure groups, and the loss of revenue to
the Treasuries of the countries concerned, with the consequent
upward pressure on public sector borrowing requirements,
frequently go unremarked except by a few financial experts.

When it comes to the provision of selective aid schemes,

however, there is frequently a barrage of complaints about 'distorting the forces of the free market' and 'creating artificial demand'. What selective aid schemes do, is permit the state to extend a form of patronage to certain classes of film and certain types of film-maker, according to the nature of the aid scheme applied for. The 'automatic' aid scheme will normally give the most financial aid to the film with the biggest domestic rental if it is an aid scheme similar to the Eady Levy. The 'selective' aid scheme will seek to support classes of films and film-makers who would otherwise find it impossible to survive.

The terms 'automatic' and 'selective' aid are ideologically loaded and confusing. Furthermore, the borderline between the two is blurred. When Great Britain set up the National Film Finance Corporation in 1949, its role was to act as the source of production finance for British films which were commercial in orientation. Its role was not to support film projects which were uncommercial. It borrowed money from the Treasury at a commercial rate of interest and was expected to make an annual profit. When the Tory government restructured its financing arrangements in 1980, there was no explicit statement that the role and the function of the NFFC were to be changed, although this took place. The role of the NFFC is now one of financing young and independent film-makers to produce what the Board of NFFC considers to be artistically exciting film projects with commercial potential. Under the new arrangements proposed in the government's White Paper, the new privatized 'son-of-NFFC' will receive £1.5 million a year to assist it to provide what the White Paper terms 'opportunities for the talented young film maker to find a foothold in the competitive world of commercial film making'. A vague phrase which covers a multitude of assumptions which are open to question, but its import is nevertheless clear. The projects must be submitted by film-makers who are 'talented', 'young' and aspire to be 'commercial', that is, those who conform to the norms of the film industry.

The funds available for film production through the NFFC, or its privatized descendant, are nevertheless small compared with the production funds which are potentially available from television. The relationship between television and the film industry varies from country to country and the opportunities for co-operation that exist vary according to the ways in which the two industries have developed side by side. In the US, as a result of the anti-trust laws, television was not permitted to produce its own fictional programmes, be they serials, series or made-for-TV films. The net outcome was that the television networks commissioned most of their fictional programmes from the Hollywood networks and today they put up some two thirds of the production finance for television films and series, while the production company is required to recoup the remaining one third of the production costs from overseas sales. Sometimes the programme will be shown in cinemas, more often they will be sold to foreign television stations. In 1976 approximately half of the film revenues of the Hollywood majors came from sales to television and about one quarter of these came from sales to overseas television networks.

In the United Kingdom and many Western European countries, a different model of television developed out of a tradition of public service broadcasting. This extended to fiction programmes as well as news and current affairs programmes. Initially the film industry, whose interests included cinema ownership, refused to sell their films to television, but the break-up of the major Hollywood film corporations following the anti-trust decision of the US Supreme Court in 1947 required them to separate production and distribution from exhibition, and the decline of the cinema as a mass market, slowly changed their attitude. In the meantime, however, the Western European television networks, rich with finance from the fast expanding sales of television licences, had developed their own drama departments. The channel controllers were able to screen old cinema films as well as their own in-house fiction productions.

As a result of the shortage of frequencies in the broadcasting spectrum, television developed as either a monopoly or duopoly in most European countries. Consequently it became possible for the broadcasters to operate within a protected market. For fictional films this worked in two ways. First, television networks were able to limit the price they were prepared to pay to film producers when they bought the television transmission rights of feature films; and second, they were able to fund the production and transmission of their own fictional programmes

– serials, series and television dramas – more generously than bought in material, most of it American. In a study carried out in 1974, it was estimated that the cost per thousand viewers of the BBC's television plays was approximately 15 times more than that of a feature film which it had bought from Hollywood.

It should not be thought, however, that the Hollywood film producers were dominated by the European television organizations. Hollywood co-ordinated its activities through an export cartel, the Motion Picture Export Association (MPEA), and the prices that it set effectively determined the going rate for the purchase of films in the world television market. The MPEA has been prepared to force television organizations to pay higher prices for its films by simply refusing to supply them with films until they agree to pay its prices, as it showed in Italy in 1973 and in Sweden in 1979. When producers claim that television is paying unreasonably low prices to screen their films, it should be borne in mind that the fees that television is paying are acceptable to the MPEA.

The television organizations of Europe have responded in different ways to the call for them to assist in funding their national film cultures. In the United Kingdom the policy has been for the BBC and ITV to build up their own drama departments, and to produce their own serials, series and television films. It is scriptwriters and directors who receive the benefits of television's patronage rather than film producers. In the Federal Republic of Germany the television organizations, many of which have substantial shareholdings in the film studios of Hamburg and Munich, have chosen to support independent film producers and directors rather than to build up their own drama departments. The much praised 'new German cinema' is essentially dependent on television finance in order to keep going. Some of the films are succesful in German cinemas, many are not. Some are successful abroad as art house films, while a few, such as Bavaria Atelier/Radiant Films' *The Boat* (Wolfgang Petersen, 1981) co-financed with West Deutscher Rundfunk and Süd Deutscher Rundfunk, are commercial successes.

In Italy the state television station, RAI, has traditionally had a policy of screening mainly informational and educational programmes and so it has developed a policy of co-financing individual film projects with a cultural orientation. It has co-financed films such as *Padre Padrone* (Paolo and Vittorio Taviani, 1976) *The Tree of the Wooden Clogs* (Ermanno Olmi, 1978) and *Nostalgia* (Andrei Tarkovsky, 1983). In recent years, however, it has been increasingly limited in the films it has been able to make. The Italian television market has become swamped by American films and television series screened by the local private television stations, which are being bought up by the major Italian publishing corporations and film distributors.

In France, where both the cinema and the television economies are much more tightly controlled by the government, there is a more complex set of arrangements between the two industries. There are limits on the number of feature films which may be shown on television each week and the television companies are required to pay sums of money into the various film aid funds which the government has set up. The franchise for the fourth television channel in France, 'Canal Plus', has been given for 12 years to the Havas Group, in which the French government is the principal shareholder. It is required to promote the cinema in a large proportion of its programmes through studying its history, transmitting films and through committing at least one quarter of its resources to financing films. In order to protect the interests of the cinema owners, films cannot be transmitted before 10 pm on Wednesdays and Fridays, before 11 pm on Saturdays, or before 8.30 pm on Sundays. At least 60 per cent of films must come from the EEC, and at least 50 per cent must have been made in the French language.

In the United Kingdom the fourth television channel, Channel Four, has been set up with a responsibility, among other things, to encourage innovation and experiment in the form and content of programmes. Since Channel Four produces no programmes of its own, unlike the BBC and the ITV companies, it has supported film production by commissioning independent film producers. The fiction films so commissioned have normally been screened in Channel Four's 'Film on Four' slot. Some of the more experimental fiction films have been broadcast in its 'At the Eleventh Hour' slot. Channel Four took the view that it could not afford to put more than £300,000 into each project, a lower sum than needed to finance most feature films, and therefore most projects need to find a co-production partner. This invariably means that there is pressure for a film to be given a cinema release before it is shown on television. The policy of the Cinematograph Exhibitors Association is not to show films unless there is an agreement for them not to be screened on television for three years, although there are exceptions for films that fail at the box office. Channel Four, however, is only prepared to accept that a film should be screened in the cinema for one year prior to its television transmission. For a television organization such as Channel Four, a cinema screening is a double-edged sword. Clearly it creates publicity for the film and can generate a lot of revenue at the box office, although the television organization will not normally benefit from that. On the other hand, if a film has too long a run at the cinema, it means that the television organization has its money tied up and it may well find that by the time it transmits the film, nearly everybody has seen it in the cinema and it will score poor audience ratings.

At the moment television finds itself at a crossroads, unsure which way to turn. Over the past decades, television organizations have built audiences and a degree of cultural autonomy at the expense of the cinema and Hollywood. Today, broadcast television finds itself in a more competitive environment, having to compete for audiences not only with the cinema but also with cable television stations and with videocassette recorders and, on the horizon, satellite broadcasting. For most governments, television organizations are primarily political organizatons whose main task is to provide an appropriate mix of news and current affairs programmes which conform to the demands of the nation's polity. Fictional programmes are simply the icing on the cake to attract the audiences for the news and current affairs programmes.

In this economic and political climate, the television organizations have to choose between attempting to grow by increasing their revenues from other sources, such as the sale of their programmes overseas and to other media including the cinema, and attempting to retain a degree of cultural and ideological autonomy over the types of projects they choose to finance. Channel Four is already having to develop a more flexible funding policy in order to balance these different demands. It currently has a long-term policy proposal to split its film finance into four categories. The first, which would give it the maximum freedom in selecting the projects it chooses to finance, would be for films which it would fund completely with amounts up to £500,000. The second would be co-productions with other European broadcasters to which Channel Four would commit between £250,000 and £300,000. The third would be pre-purchasing agreements to buy the television rights for three screenings of a film which would cost up to £250,000. The fourth and last category would be to invest in mainstream commercial projects sums up to £750,000 of which it would aim to recover at least £500,000 from other markets as an investor. Channel Four is no longer simply a patron of British film-makers, it is also attempting to become a film banker, which explains its readiness to become a shareholder in the new privatized NFFC.

The other main source of state patronage in the UK is the Production Board of the British Film Institute. It was originally set up in 1953 as the Experimental Film Fund of the Institute, but over the years its finances have grown. In the 1970 Films Act it was enabled to receive funds from the Eady Levy and since that time it has received an annual grant from Eady which has risen from £10,000 in 1971 to £125,000 in 1984. In their White Paper the Tory government have proposed the abolition of the Eady Levy, thus ending the Board's supply of funds from that source. The BFI Production Board has other sources of funds however. In 1984 it had a budget of £923,000. Of this, £350,000 came from Channel Four, £400,000 from the Office of Arts and Libraries and £48,000 from The Independent Television Companies Association (ITCA).

Although the prime purpose of the BFI Production Board is not regarded as being that of making feature films, it has had a long flirtation with the cinema and with low budget feature films. Many feature film directors started their careers with the Board, for example Karel Reisz, Tony Richardson, Ken Russell, Lindsay Anderson, Jack Gold, Chris Petit and Peter Greenaway. Conversely many of the films that it has produced have also had cinema release. Its biggest commercial success was the stylish avant-garde feature film *The Draughtsman's Contract* (Peter Greenaway, 1983), although strictly speaking the film hasn't yet covered its costs. The basic budget for the film was £305,000 and the residuals for the crew, who worked at minimun rates under a special agreement with ACTT, increase this to £425,000. Although the UK cinema rentals were £124,000 most of this went in prints and publicity costs. To date the BFI has picked up £150,000 from a screening on Channel Four, and £205,000 from advance sales to the USA, Europe and Australia.

Over the years the Production Board has financed other low budget feature films which have been shown in art house cinemas and on television. In some cases it has entered into co-production arrangements with foreign film companies or foreign television stations, but in all cases it has remained crucially dependent on state finance to continue to balance its books. This being so, the main controversies surrounding the projects which the Production Board has chosen to support have centred on the extent to which it should attempt to fund projects destined for cinema release and the extent to which it should attempt to fund other projects such as documentaries or avant-garde and experimental projects. The current position is that it attempts to fund a mixture of all three, but its funds are so limited that it barely manages to fund one project from each category in a given year.

The arguments which surround the BFI Production Board and its funding policies stem from a distinction which is increasingly being made between 'the film' and 'the cinema'. Traditionally the only type of film which has been shown in cinemas has been the feature film, together with the occasional short film, or newsreel. On television however, we are used to seeing a range of programmes, many of which are made on film. Some were originally designed for cinema releases, others were made by the television company. There is no longer a clear distinction between a cinema film and a television film. Even the distinction between 'fiction' and 'documentary' which the television companies have tried to maintain for so long, is becoming blurred. Film-makers have realized and have come to exploit the fact that *all* film-makers both record images of events that are actually taking place and then edit these individual shots together to create the illusion that they can be fitted together to form a coherent narrative. In the feature film the reality which is recorded is that of actors and actresses speaking the words written by someone else; in the documentary film the reality which is recorded is the real world as observed by the camera, although the presence of the camera, the point of view or the framing of the shot may well give us a false impression of what is happening. In the feature film the narrative is constructed and pre-planned by a professional scriptwriter; in the documentary the narrative that is constructed, often with the aid of a commentary, is one that purports to explain to us the events that are recorded by the camera in terms which the film-maker considers make sense.

This realization that film is a complex artefact which hovers somewhere on the borderline between the real and the imaginary, has meant that both film-makers, and the more discerning members of the audience, have begun to seek to look at films in other contexts than simply sitting in the cinema or passively watching television. The videocassette recorder has given us all the means to stop a film, to rewind it and to examine it in detail. No longer is a film something which rolls unceasingly from beginning to end. Many films are now shown in other contexts such as film societies, the classroom, or to clubs and groups. They are seen for a specific purpose which goes beyond entertainment. Crucial to these developments are not only the increased opportunities provided by new technology, but also the new insights being developed in film education. It is to these that I now want to turn.

10. Education

The cinema began life as a mass medium. What the film trade wanted was for its films to be seen by as many people as possible, and as quickly as possible. In this manner a film could make the maximum profit from the marketplace and there would be a continuous demand for a regular flow of films produced by the studios. In short, the film trade wanted the public to become regular consumers.

There were others, however, who realized that film had different qualities. Some people were concerned to emphasize the artistic qualities of the new medium, others the impact of film on people's social awareness or behaviour. When the first Films Act was passed in Great Britain in 1927 it carefully avoided any consideration of the quality of British films and as a result there were many who felt that there was a gap in British social and cultural life which was not filled by the 'quota quickies', the cheap British films that were being made in order to obtain the maximum economic benefits from the Films Act.

One group which wanted to develop an appreciation of the art of the film, and also to bypass the BBFC's draconian strictures on some foreign films, established The Film Society as a venue where people could see and discuss films which were different from those shown in popular cinemas, such as classic Soviet films like *Battleship Potemkin* and *Storm Over Asia*, or non-fiction films produced by film-makers such as the documentary group working for the Empire Marketing Board. Other film societies were set up outside London along the same lines, many of which showed the same films, and a national movement was born.

Others were more concerned about the specific content of films. For them it was not enough for the BBFC to cut out the worst parts of commercial feature films. What they wanted was to use all the communication possibilities that the film offered for educational, instructional and morally uplifting purposes, in schools, colleges and elsewhere.

The final outcome of this division in British social and cultural life between the film trade and those who saw other possibilities for film was the setting up in 1933 of The British Film Institute whose aim was 'to encourage the art of the film' but whose constitution prevented it from involving itself in matters connected with the film trade or in matters concerning film censorship. As well as developing a National Film Archive and the National Film Theatre, the BFI attracted a number of people who were concerned with the relationships between film and education. In 1949 the British Film Institute Act was passed which enabled the BFI to receive an annual grant from the Treasury, which is now its principal source of funds. In 1983 it received a Royal Charter. In the early days, many concerns of the BFI were primarily technical and were linked to the possibilities of showing in the classroom 16 millimetre versions of cinema films and of technical, instructional and documentary films. The film societies, too, were concerned with the possibilities of using 16 millimetre prints to show to their members, and gradually a small but significant market in 16 millimetre film rentals was developed, aimed at both film societies and schools and colleges.

The hire of feature films was, however, a very expensive item for most schools and colleges, and little serious or educational work emerged until the 1960s when a number of significant developments occurred in parallel, leading to a massive explosion in film education. The key developments were the growth of relatively cheap 16 millimetre production technology, combined with the educational resources to exploit it; the establishment by the Labour Government of a national network of Polytechnics with degrees validated by the Council for National Academic Awards (CNAA) and the emergence at the BFI of an Educational Advisory Service which was able to nurture and encourage much of the best theoretical and academic study of film and make it available to teachers and lecturers in education to draw on it and develop it for their own work.

In the early part of the 1960s, colleges concentrated on developing film courses that were mainly practical in aim, encouraging students simply to imitate the conventions of the commercial industry, or alternatively to pursue an art college tradition of personal creative expression. The setting up of the new polytechnics and the need to gain the approval of the CNAA in order to award a degree, meant that many colleges developed courses which offered a mix of theoretical and practical studies. There were also strong economic arguments against the continuation and expansion of purely practical courses. Although colleges had invested in equipment for film production such as cameras, editing machines and dubbing consoles, they also had to meet substantial costs each year to pay for film stock and laboratory processing charges. Furthermore, the government had established the National Film School in 1970 (now the National Film and Television School) which had the specific responsibility for training professional film-makers.

It was from this background that film education emerged, and within it the need for a coherent body of knowledge and criteria for the analysis and study of films, which could turn the unreflective film consumer into a reflective and discerning critic who could not only enjoy the very real and sensual pleasures which the cinema offered, but also reflect upon and respond to those films in a positive and productive manner. A number of key areas of concern were therefore developed within film study, which were designed to assist the student in achieving these aims at all levels, from CSE and O Level to undergraduate and even postgraduate studies. One of these areas is a concern with realism and with the ability of the cinema to portray a world which both purports to be real and which is at the same time clearly imaginary. How are we to disentangle what is 'real' in a film and what is 'imaginary'? How far is what we see typical of reality and to what extent does it express a wider truth about the condition of the society it purports to portray? Does this illusion of reality which the film offers have a social role or purpose, or alternatively can it be used for social progress? These and other questions take us into related areas of study.

One of these is to consider the very way in which film expression is articulated. Traditionally, film theorists assumed that there was something called 'film language', but recently this has been called into question by showing that the so-called film language has been socially determined by the institution of cinema itself which brought together a number of economic, social and psychological requirements which classical 'film language' met through the form in which it developed.

Alongside these more general and theoretical studies, film study also includes the study of the role of individual film-makers working within the system. The means whereby an individual creative consciousness can express itself, either through the script or through the non-verbal codes of the *mise-en-scène* such as the design of the set, the costumes, the framing or the lighting of the image, or through the deployment of music or of camera movement. These lead to a more general consideration of the relationship between the individual artist working in the film production process and the nature of film production itself. Against this area of enquiry, film studios have also looked at alternative traditions of film-making which draw on different cultural traditions such as the European art film and modernist and avant-garde experimental productions. These areas of enquiry call into question the traditional modes of representation adopted by Hollywood and the mainstream film industries. A final area of study is one which is precisely concerned with the psychological relationships between the film viewer and the film text. It encompasses both broad-scale studies of the social impact of film and detailed analyses of the psychological operations of individual film texts.

Naturally all of these areas of study interpenetrate and interweave with each other. The study of film is a multifaceted and a multidisciplinary activity which parallels the richness and the density of the film medium itself. It is now clear, however, that film education is beginning to have a number of significant effects which cannot fail to influence the very nature of cinema itself.

One of these has been to create a more diversified and more stratified audience for films. Whereas the film trade seeks to establish a mass audience for films, film education is producing minority audiences with different cultural and educational backgrounds and expectations. On occasion these different audiences may go to see the same film, but they may well come away with significantly different interpretations of it. Some may simply enjoy the content of the film for what it is, or enjoy the pleasures it offers in an uncritical manner. Others will try to disentangle the different creative contributions which have gone into the film by looking for the authorial 'marks' of different technicians. Yet others will be asking how realistic a view the film gives of the real world or of human nature. A fourth group may be attempting to uncover the psychological operation of the film, trying to assess how the narrative or the expressive language of the film corral and release our unconscious repressions. And so on. Of course many of these activities may be taking place simultaneously in the same person's head. It is possible to enjoy the simple emotional pleasures of a film and to think about it critically at the same time.

As we have already seen, the cinema has had to face up to the decline of the mass audience and it can therefore no longer rely on the habit audience for its profits, but at the same time it has seen the possibility of increased admissions from an audience which is more concerned with questions of art and culture. But the changes go further than that for they raise questions both about the nature of film censorship and about the very relationship of the cinema to film viewing.

First, censorship. Although the film trade has always preferred to present films as being aimed at mass audience, in reality there have always been different audiences for the same film, as the censors have to admit. According to a pamphlet which it published in the 1930s, the criteria which the BBFC used when censoring films were based on the impression which the film would make on an average audience which in its opinion included 'a not inconsiderable proportion of people of immature judgement'. This was interpreted to mean a not inconsiderable proportion of the working class. It was therefore left to the radical intelligentsia of the 1930s to build up the film society movement where people who were seriously interested in the art of the film could show both art films and films of a socialist political persuasion which had been produced overseas. The Masses Film and Stage Guild was refused permission by the London County Council to show the Russian film *Mother* (Vsevolod Pudovkin, 1926), even though it had already been shown by The Film Society. The reason given was that whereas the subscription to The Film Society was 25 shillings, that for the Masses Film and Stage Guild was only one shilling, and therefore the film was in the reach of everyone.

After the Second World War, the BBFC became more

sophisticated in its judgements and more lenient towards art house films than films aimed at a mass market. Today, however, the political climate has changed, and with the enactment of the Video Recordings Act extending the arm of the censor to video recordings, the only area of film distribution which is not pre-censored is the 16 millimetre distribution of films which are shown in schools, colleges and to private clubs, societies or other associations. The net outcome of these changes in censorship arrangements is that it is now mainly the educators and those who are being educated who are permitted to see uncensored films, and it is possible to anticipate a division developing in society similar to that which existed in the 1930s between an intellectual elite and the mass of people.

This same division is likely to be intensified by the tastes and the awareness of audiences who have studied film in a formal way as part of their education. One of the reasons why people pursue courses of study is to differentiate themselves from others by equipping themselves with specialist knowledge or specialist skills. The formal study of film in an educational context can provide both but, more than that, it can give the student additional pleasures in watching films that are not immediately apparent to the uneducated eye. The challenge, to both society and the world of education, is to permit film education to develop in a manner which is socially productive and not socially divisive, and which enables audiences both to continue to enjoy the basic physical, sensual and psychological pleasures that the cinema can offer, and at the same time to be aware of how the cinema operates in society, and the dangers and the misuses to which it can fall victim. In this way the cinema changes from being them talking to us, it starts to become the medium through which a society addresses itself, not just about reality but also about its hopes and its fears, its dreams and its nightmares, its aspirations and its despairs.

These ideals for cinema will not be achieved easily. There are some tentative moves in this direction, but there are also some very solid obstacles which are standing in the way of progress. How they are to be negotiated raises major political as well as social and ideological questions.

Perhaps the main question now on the agenda is that of cultural democracy. When cinema developed its classic form it took in Hollywood before the Second World War, it was argued that it was the law of the free market that should determine which films we should see in our cinemas. Most countries objected to the fact that their screens were dominated by Hollywood films and introduced various legislative and financial arrangements to protect the free market for their own national and cultural ends. The arrival of television complicated matters, and the advent of new technologies will certainly complicate matters even more.

As we have seen, the types of film that we see on our screens, is inseparable from the ways in which they are financed and distributed, and yet these are matters which are usually beyond the control not only of the people who watch them, but also of national governments. What the cinema offers us in return for our admission fee is a pleasurable illusion for two or three hours. Once we have paid our money, we have no say in our cultural future. The cinema is a one-way transmission system from the film corporation to us. The only way in which we can show our objection is to get up and leave the cinema. If the cinema is to become a medium through which a society talks to itself about its concerns we have to think seriously about ways of changing a massively centralized system with a one-way flow of ideas, emotions attitudes and experiences, into a genuinely flexible communication system.

Education is a process in which we can teach ourselves to come to terms with the cinema, not simply by talking about it, but also by setting out to change it, so that we too can have a say not just in the films that we see, but also in the films that are made. This requires a proper recognition of cultural differences and of cultural diversity, not only in terms of nationality and/or region, but also in terms of class, gender and race. It means identifying and nurturing our cultural resources and ensuring that they have an opportunity to express not simply their ideas and emotions, but also our ideas and emotions. It means not simply sitting and looking at films, but discussing them, and looking at them more than once, with new eyes as well as old. It means making our own films as well as looking at those of the movie majors.

11. Changes

To make any changes in the institution of cinema is an extremely difficult and complex matter. It involves not only economics, but also aspects of social policy, social psychology, the cultural and class divisions in society and educational policy. At its very root is the question of cultural democracy. How is it possible for a society to determine for itself the forces which provide it with its entertainments and its pleasures, its daydreams and its nightmares, its aspirations and its fears?

Over the years, there have been many attempts to legislate and control the cinema, and even more proposals which have been ignored. Despite these attempts, there have been relatively few changes in the major corporations which dominate the fields of film production and distribution. Before the Second World War, the screens of the world were dominated by films from MGM, Warner Brothers, Twentieth Century Fox, Columbia, Universal, Paramount, United Artists and RKO. Today all of those companies, except RKO, continue to dominate the screens of the world. To be sure, there have been periods of ups and downs for individual companies, but in the long term, there has been a remarkable consistency in the companies which have dominated the cinema. Why has this been so?

Although these corporations are frequently thought of as being American, they are in fact multi-national corporations based in America. This means that they take a global view of the cinema markets of the world, and in addition they have the resources and the ability to produce their films in whichever country suits their own financial interests. Key technicians can be bought and flown from one country to another to produce films in those places which best suit the corporate needs. Hollywood, where the companies produce most of their films, is an international colony which includes many British, German,

French and other technicians. In their view of the cinema, the concept of a national culture is meaningless. Films are produced by technicians and creative personnel who come from many different countries and they are marketed and exhibited internationally.

But most of the major film corporations are also subsidiaries of even larger corporate conglomerates. Universal is a subsidiary of the giant Music Corporation of America (MCA), Paramount is a subsidiary of Gulf and Western, and Twentieth Century Fox a subsidiary of Rupert Murdoch's News Corporation. In Great Britain too the major film corporations are subsidiaries of even larger organizations. Thorn-EMI Screen Entertainment (TESE) is a subsidiary of the giant Thorn-EMI group, and Goldcrest is a subsidiary of the Pearson Group which owns among other things Penguin Books, Longmans, the Financial Times and Madame Tussauds. The reason most of the film corporations have been taken over by larger groups, has been primarily financial. But financial controls can also lead to creative controls. When United Artists was taken over by the Trans-america Corporation, the top officers of United Artists – Arthur Krim, Robert Benjamin and Eric Pleskow – found that slowly but surely Transamerica was placing more and more restrictions on them, even though their films were commercially successful. Three of the five films nominated for Oscars in 1976 were United Artists' pictures – *Rocky*, *Network* and *Bound For Glory*; one, *Rocky*, was the winner. Despite this, Transamerica's pressures continued to mount. Finally, Krim, Benjamin and Pleskow resigned as a group, to set up Orion Pictures.

One of the advantages of large corporations from the point of view of the senior management, is the way in which different subsidiary companies can act together to mould and shape the markets. Most film companies have affiliated book and record publishing companies. It has been well known for many years that people who have read books, will often want to see the film of the book and that people who have seen the film, will often want to buy the book of the film. A similar relationship exists between a film and the record of its soundtrack. Not surprisingly the major film corporations set out to exploit these connections by using their book publishing affiliates to assist in marketing their film with book sales and to generate additional profits from sales of the book of the film, and by using their record affiliates in a similar manner. Other spin-offs such as toys, T-shirts, key-rings, and computer games are also manufactured and marketed as part of these promotional campaigns.

Naturally these massive co-ordinated marketing campaigns not only have a commercial impact, generating substantial profits for the multinational parent conglomerates, but they also have a massive impact on people's cultural life. Take for example the recent movie history of breakdancing. It began life on the outskirts of New York as part of an oppositional adolescent culture in which the ethnic minorities, the underprivileged and the poor of Reagan's America channelled their energies into ironic parodies of conventional art forms. Breakdancing, together with record 'scratching' and the graffiti art of the New York subway, were shown for what they are – an oppositional folk culture – in the semi-documentary *Wild Style* (Charlie Ahearn, 1982) made by a small independent company, Wildstyle Productions. This charming film gained a certain underground reputation, and the major companies were not slow to exploit the new folk culture for all it was worth. In doing so, however, they played up those elements of the new culture that suited their own commercial interests and played down those which they saw as a threat. Whereas *Wild Style* had centred on the activities of a New York graffiti artist and his rivals, illegally painting their names on the subway trains at night in order to 'light up the line', in Orion's *Beat Street* (Stan Lathan, 1984) the subway graffiti art is marginalized and the character at the centre of the narrative is a DJ, who raps with his discs. Whereas in *Wild Style* the breakdancing, although definitely a part of the plot, is relatively insignificant, in *Beat Street* it becomes central. In Cannon's *Breakdance* (Joel Silberg, 1984) breakdancing is distanced even further from graffiti art. The film is situated in Venice, California rather than New York, and graffiti art doesn't even appear, while in Cannon's *Breakdance 2 – Electric Boogaloo* (Sam Firstenberg, 1985) the move of breakdancing from being part of an oppositional culture to being part of a capitalist culture is completed. The central concern of the narrative is whether or not the main characters can raise enough money to set up a breakdance club.

This ideological shift from oppositional culture to capitalist culture was naturally accompanied by spin-off profits from the sales of records and tapes of the films concerned. Whereas the soundtrack of *Wild Style* was not issued separately, *Beat Street* was a multi-media marketing operation, and its soundtrack was marketed separately on tape and disc by the Atlantic Recording Corporation, a subsidiary of Warner Communications, thus creating a multi-media push for the film and the disc simultaneously. There were similar arrangements for the two *Breakdance* films. The effect of this cultural marketing operation, spearheaded by the release of the films, was twofold. First, it selected one element from an oppositional urban culture which sprang out of the intense economic, racial and social pressures which existed in some of the ghettos in New York, and sanitized and fetishized one element – breakdancing – for its own commercial purposes, thus making huge profits for the shareholders of the corporations concerned. And second, it deformed and twisted a vibrant cultural opposition to the worst excesses of capitalism, into a commercialized cultural fad, restricted to a few elite performers and completely separated from its cultural origins.

It is virtually impossible for a country to resist these assaults on its cultural life. To attempt either to ban the films and their associated books and records or to censor the films would probably prove counter-productive. In the former case, to ban the entry of the films would be counter to the rules of GATT which regulate trade between capitalist countries and would, in the long term, force the offending country to leave both GATT and the European Economic Community. Any attempt to censor the films would raise a major question about the commercial and political accountability of film censorship and would be in grave danger of leading to an authoritarian control of film taste. Film policy basically has to choose between preventing certain films from being shown, on the one hand, and supporting and encouraging new developments on the other.

A clear example of the policy of preventing films from being shown, is the 1984 Video Recordings Act, which makes the basic assumption that every videotape is potentially evil and obscene and must therefore be censored before it can be seen by the public. To implement this act, the BBFC has expended its bureaucracy considerably and the United Kingdom is slowly but steadily moving further down the road towards a totalitarian and centralized form of film and video censorship. Under the arrangements for cinema censorship, these powers were delegated to local authorities so that there was the possibility of a plurality of decisions. The arrangements for video censorship however are centralized within one body, nominated by the Home Secretary.

The expanding bureaucracy of censorship will, of course, have to be paid for, and the people who will pay are the distributors who have to have their films and videos censored before they can show them to the public. The current proposal is for the BBFC to charge a minimum of £2.00 per minute for any film which has already been censored for cinema release, and double that figure for a film which has not. This means that any person who produces a video lasting for 90 minutes, the running time of an average feature film, will have to pay a censorship fee of £360. For a major commercial distributor this level of fee may be acceptable, but for the small independent producer, a fee of this size is a substantial obstacle which must be overcome before the film can be distributed. The net result of the 1984 Video Recordings Act will be to discriminate adversely against the small, independent film and video producer.

The new developments in film and cinema, on the other hand, may be encouraged in a number of ways. The traditional British policy has been one of supporting the film industry rather than individual films. The cinema quota, the Eady Levy and the National Film Finance Corporation were all measures designed to support and develop a national film industry which would produce films to be shown in cinemas alongside those of Hollywood. As we have seen, this policy makes little sense today. Many films which were legally British such as Alexander and Ilya Salkind's *Superman* (Richard Donner, 1978), *Superman II* (Richard Lester, 1981) and *Superman III* (Richard Lester, 1983) are simply international films which happen to be made in Britain. The concept of a British company becomes an increasingly meaningless one, since most major film companies are effectively multinational companies. US based multinationals shoot their films in Hollywood, Pinewood or Borehamwood, whichever is the cheapest and most convenient. British multinationals have the same attitude.

The decision to abolish the Eady Levy on cinema seats is long overdue, but not surprisingly both the film producers and the ACTT want it to be replaced by a similar redistributive levy, possibly based on the sale of films to television and the sale or hire of pre-recorded videocassettes. At first sight, this proposal seems attractive in that it continues to offer a financial incentive to international film producers to make their films in Great Britain. There are however a number of major problems with this proposal. The first is that other factors can offer film producers a more substantial incentive for producing their films in Great Britain. The main ones are the value of the pound in the international currency markets and the real labour costs, measured in US dollars, necessary for producing the film. The second is that such a policy will switch resources from the television industry which has some degree of permanent employment, to the feature film industry which is totally casualized. It will mean the expansion within the ACTT of a casualized work force who will see their interests as being the same as those of international film producers and the ideologies that they espouse. A third danger is that there is a real likelihood of a competitive race developing between states to offer film producers more and more incentives. Within the US nearly every one of the 50 states has a motion picture office whose role is to attract film-makers. Although most of the major film studios remain in California, more and more films are being shot on location, and the financial incentives offered to film-makers to shoot their films in another state can include reductions in state taxes, preferential deals on accommodation, transport, communications and, in some states, free access to the resources of the police and fire departments. Representatives of these motion picture offices even make special visits to London to try to persuade British film producers to shoot their films on the other side of the Atlantic.

Another hope of British film producers is that the preferential tax arrangements for film financing which were abolished in the 1984 budget, will be brought back. Here again there is a danger that countries will compete with one another to provide more and better tax incentives than their rivals. These simply redistribute money to film production and away from other activities which are funded by the state such as health and education programmes. There is also growing evidence that as the new film markets open up, be they cable, satellite or videocassette, investors are prepared to finance the production of films for them without these incentives. In May 1984 Goldcrest Film and Television raised £22 million from the stock market and the offer was oversubscribed. Thorn-EMI Screen Entertainment (TESE) issued £36 million shares to UK city investors in December 1984 for participation in the funding of five future productions, and the UK film leasing company Albion Films has recently launched a major new investment plan for UK and European investors to co-finance films with the major Hollywood studios. In this financial climate, tax concessions to the film industry hardly seem necessary.

Against these undiscriminating policies of support for the film industry, we may set policies which seek to encourage the production of films which are qualitatively different from those normally produced by the commercial film industry. In recent years both the NFFC and the BFI Production Board have attempted to finance film production in this manner. There are really two choices available here. One is to try and co-finance film projects with the commercial sector (a policy largely pursued by the NFFC), the other is to try and finance film projects on one's own (a policy largely pursued by the BFI Production Board). In both instances the state funding bodies almost always failed to get any commercial return for their investment, but their investment acted as a form of hidden subsidy for the co-financier, for the film distributor and for the film exhibitor. If the projects which the state body attempts to support are not backed by the commercial sector they do not normally get off the ground, a problem that the NFFC has had to recognize in recent years, since many projects which it encouraged were unable to find additional sources of finance and thus fell by the wayside.

The way in which the current Conservative Government is attempting to reconcile this contradiction between the judgement of commercial investors and the state support for film, is simply to hand the selection of projects over to the commercial sector and to subsidize the commercial sector directly. The NFFC is to be replaced by a new private company, The British Screen Finance Consortium, in which Channel Four, Thorn-EMI,

Rank and the British Videogram Association (BVA) will be the main partners. They will put up £1.1 million for film financing and in return the government will put up £1.5 million. Together with the profits arising from the exploitation of the assets of old NFFC films, this will give the new consortium approximately £3 million to invest each year in approximately ten low-budget films.

While this solution will prevent differences of opinion arising as to which projects to support, there is no guarantee that the films supported by the new consortium will be any different from those made within the industry. In the government White Paper there was talk of the need to commission unknown film-makers, but this does not appear to be a requirement for the Consortium to carry on receiving public subsidy. There are also very real questions about the ways in which both public money and state-owned assets are being transferred to the public sector. It would appear that the main partners in the Consortium are getting a very good deal from the government as part of its privatization programme. It may well be, however, that some of the films financed by the Consortium are interesting and different. The participation of Channel Four as one of the partners may well be beneficial and the consortium also has the strength that all of its partners have direct access through their subsidiaries to the audio-visual market. Rank and Thorn-EMI both own cinema chains, are major shareholders in commercial television stations and have interests in cable television. Channel Four has, of course, its own television network, while the BVA represents the interests of the major suppliers of videocassettes.

Access for new and independent films to the cinema screen has been one of the major commercial barriers to setting up a film policy which produces films which are qualitatively different. The changes proposed by the Monopolies and Mergers Commission, whereby a popular film should not be exhibited for more than four weeks unless the film is made available to all other cinemas in effective competition with the original cinema, are hardly likely to encourage the wider showing of alternative films in circuit cinemas. The government intends to conduct an experiment for a period of one year in Manchester and Glasgow and it will be interesting to see the effects of the proposal, not only on the showing of popular films but also on the showing of minority films.

An alternative cinema policy which has been developed in France under the Mitterrand administration is one which attempts to reverse the trend towards fewer and centralized cinemas by setting up an agency to develop regional cinema. The Agency for Regional Cinema Development uses government funds to develop new film exhibition centres in rural areas, in small towns and in the suburbs of large ones. A twin-pronged strategy has been developed. One strand provides the places for the films to be shown, the other strand makes sure that prints are available to the films the public wants to see. A careful examination of the map of France showed the areas where there was a shortage of cinemas. Money was then made available to develop and support local initiatives such as opening a new cinema, renovating an old one or twinning a single screen cinema. The Agency also provides know-how on matters such as basic cinema management, financial projections and the promotion and development of publicity activities.

The second strand involves working with film distributors by buying additional copies of major commercial releases to supply provincial and regional cinemas as soon as possible after the Paris release of the film. The decline of many regional and provincial cinemas, it was argued, had been accelerated by the inability of smaller cinemas to obtain prints of the major commercial successes when they were first released, and audiences had preferred to watch television rather than go to the cinema to watch outdated films – an argument which is echoed by the independent cinemas in Great Britain.

The Agency for Regional Development has been a notable success, but it has also aroused much hostility. It has been accused of using government money to subsidize popular films, of buying prints which it then shows in the cinemas it supports before other cinemas can get their regular supply of prints from the commercial distributors, and of encouraging a system which depends on the expenditure of substantial publicity costs to launch a film. It has also been pointed out that it makes no sense for the government to subsidize regional cinemas while at the same time giving the go-ahead for a national commercial television channel – Canal Plus.

The contradiction which exists in France between subsidizing the cinema and developing other outlets for films exists in other countries too. The cinema, television, cable television, satellites and videocassettes all want to show similar films. Films which are qualitatively different need different conditions of production and alternative modes of exhibition. One way in which this is being achieved in Great Britain is through the development of film workshops. This policy was developed by independent film-makers working within the film trade union ACTT, partly as an attempt to resist the increased casualization of employment in the industry and partly from a recognition that the independent 'film-maker' was in reality dependent on sources of finance, and that it was shortage of finance that stifled creative opportunities.

The film workshop agreement which was established three years ago, was signed by ACTT, the BFI, the film and television officers of the regional arts associations and the Independent Film-makers Association (now the IFVA). It permits smaller production crews and lower salaries than is normal in the casualized film industry and is designed to encourage the growth and development of non-profit-making co-operatives funded by various grant-giving bodies such as the BFI, the regional arts associations, Channel Four and local authorities. The co-operatives are required to be under the democratic control of their members, to pay regular wages and to permit flexible working between different grades. In addition, film workshops are expected to promote a spread of cultural activities such as film screenings, educational meetings and discussions which are related to film. To date 11 workshops have been recognized by the ACTT, nine of them receiving assistance from Channel Four.

Since they were established, the film workshops have produced a range of films which are substantially different in character and in quality. Many of them have been shown on Channel Four. Naturally most of the films produced have been shorts and documentaries such as Cinema Action's *So That You Can Live*, the Birmingham Film And Video Workshop's *Home Taping* or the Sheffield Film Co-op's *Red Skirts On Clydeside*. Front Room Productions, however, managed (within the workshop agreement) to produce a feature film *Acceptable Levels*

(John Davis, 1983) which looks at the problems involved in the TV reporting of the situation in Northern Ireland.

Despite the imaginative and radical initiative of the film workshop agreement the future looks bleak. Channel Four's decision to become a partner in The British Screen Finance Consortium, and the Conservative government's attempts to restrict public sector expenditure which affects both the BFI, and, via the Arts Council, the regional arts associations, and its proposals to ratecap local authorities, are all moves which threaten the funding sources of the film-workshops, narrowing the opportunities for alternative film finance and concentrating resources in major commercial organizations. A key factor in all this will be the way in which Channel Four distributes its resources between The British Screen Finance Consortium and the alternative film-makers working within the conditions of the film-workshop agreement.

Whichever way you turn, there are disadvantages to most of the policies which have been advanced to change the cinema. The radical aspect of the ACTT's film workshop policy is not only that it creates a range of workshops where new types of film culture can be developed – albeit on a limited scale – but it also offers a way in which the film-makers can establish a relationship with their audiences which is different to that which the traditional cinema fosters. It is frequently argued that the cinema is superior to television because it is a social activity which gets people out of the home and into the cinema, but we need to examine carefully what that means. Although people get out of the domestic environment, the pleasures, the emotions and the assumptions that they take from films shown in the cinema are rarely discussed and almost never examined. What the new emergent film workshops offer is a way in which the film-makers can open up a dialogue with audiences and with their local community about the experiences offered both by their own films and by the films of others.

The ordinary cinema is in decline and cannot continue to pay its way. As the Agency for Regional Development has shown in France, with an appropriate strategy of government support, people can be encouraged to come back to the cinema and it is clear that there is still substantial public demand for the popular film. It has also become clear, however, even to commercial cinema operators, that the cinema cannot continue to live on a diet of commercial films alone. One of the ways forward is for the cinema to turn itself into a multi-purpose cultural centre offering restaurant and bar facilities, maybe a small videothèque, a discussion room, and perhaps even production facilities which could house the local film workshop. During 1983 the clubroom of the National Film Theatre generated an income of nearly £1 million, marginally more than its film screenings, and the BFI itself made grants of some £200,000 to regional cinemas and film theatres from its Housing the Cinema fund. Other grants to film workshops and regional arts associations have assisted in the development of regional centres in different parts of the United Kingdom.

The cinema cultural centre which brings together the screenings of films, a social and cultural environment where they can be discussed, and the opportunity for local film workshops to grow and develop, means that it is possible to develop a film culture which has more interaction between film-makers and audiences than is currently possible. If the cinema, and indeed television, wants to lay claim to being a cultural activity in any genuine sense then it must recognize that its audiences must play a significant role in its development. This cannot be achieved in the traditional way in which the cinema is organized. If the cinema requires public money, then it must be accountable to the public which provides that money.

One way in which it must become accountable, as I have argued, is to permit arrangements, such as the film workshop agreement, which encourage alternative ways of making films and which produce different types of film. A second way in which it must become accountable is by moving towards different arrangements for showing films, where the old-style dream palace gradually becomes a multi-purpose cultural centre housing not just film screenings, but other activities such as discussions, videoscreenings and small-scale local production facilities. The third and final way in which the cinema must become more accountable is for the film corporations to release the tight hold which they have over the ways in which their films are used once they have been completed, and the only way in which this can be done is to change the laws of copyright.

At the present time the film-maker, and this means the large film corporation as well as the struggling independent film author, has total control not only over the way in which the whole film is used but over the way in which each section, even each frame, is used. Originally the intention was not unreasonable. It was that the film-maker should not be deprived of legitimate returns for showing the film and should be able to prevent the film being copied illegally. Today, however, some corporations extend their powers beyond this. Some films are withdrawn from circulation in order to create a space in the marketplace for a new product. On other occasions prohibitively high prices are charged for the screening of a film in a non-profit making situation. A way has to be found of giving the film user, as well as the film-maker, a say in how and when films can be shown.

One way of doing this would be to look at the rights which are granted to people who want to use printed material, such as books' or journal articles. Every reader has the right to make a copy for the purposes of private study and research or to cite extracts for the purposes of criticism or review: there are also additional rights for using material in educational institutions. These rights should be extended to audiovisual material. It should be possible for an individual to make their own videocopy of a film for private study without breaking the law. It should be possible for a film-maker to cite extracts from another film when making an audiovisual essay. And finally, it should be possible for an educational institution to run courses in film and television studies without either being severely limited in the films they can show to their students or having to pay unreasonably large sums to show them.

When all these aims have been achieved, then the cinema will have ceased to be an institution purveying the dreams, pleasures and the ideologies of capitalism. It will have the potential to become a geniunely cultural activity which is both more pluralist in its forms and more accountable in the way in which it is organized.

Suggestions For Further Reading

Your local library should be able to obtain any book on this list without difficulty.

Rachel Low, *The History of the British Film*, George Allen & Unwin, London: Vol. 1, *1896-1908* (with Roger Manvell), 1948; Vol. 2, *1908-1914*, 1949; Vol. 3, *1914-1918*, 1950; Vol. 4, *1918-1929*, 1971; *1929-39 Films of Comment and Persuasion*, 1979; *1929-39 Documentary and Educational Films of the 1930s*, 1979; *1929-39 Film-making in 1930s Britain*, 1985. A full and well-documented account of the cinema in Great Britain prior to the Second World War. It relies heavily on trade sources.

James Curran and Vincent Porter (eds), *British Cinema History*, Weidenfeld & Nicholson, (London: 1983). A collection of 19 essays which surveys the ownership, control, structure and content of British cinema from its beginnings until the 1980s. Many essays contain material not available elsewhere.

Jeffrey Richards, *The Age of the Dream Palace, Cinema and Society in Britain, 1930-1939*, Routledge & Kegan Paul (London: 1984). An in-depth study of an important decade in British cinema.

Margaret Dickinson and Sarah Street, *Cinema and State, The Film Industry and the British Government 1927-84*, British Film Institute (London: 1985). A blow-by-blow account of the battle to protect the British film industry from US domination.

Raymond Durgnat, *A Mirror For England: British Movies from Austerity to Affluence*, Faber & Faber (London: 1970). An idiosyncratic survey of British films between 1940 and 1970. Incisive, insightful and frequently annoying. Well worth reading.

Alexander Walker, *Hollywood England*, Michael Joseph (London: 1974). A good journalistic account of how Hollywood colonized the British film industry in the 1950s and 1960s.

Michael Chanan, *The Dream that Kicks: the Prehistory and Early Years of Cinema in Britain*, Routledge & Kegan Paul, (London: 1980). A Marxist reassessment of the prehistory of cinema emphasizing the extent to which it was formed from the growing forces of 19th-century capitalism and the influences of both working-class and middle-class culture.

Gorham Kindem (ed.), *The American Movie Industry: The Business of Motion Pictures*, Southern Illinois University Press (Carbondale and Edwardsville: 1982). A collection of 18 essays which together make up an economic and legal history of the American film industry.

Janet Wasko, *Movies and Money: Financing the American Film Industry*, Ablex Publishing Corporation (Norwood, New Jersey: 1982). The changing relations between Hollywood and the banks from the beginning until 1980.

Thomas H. Guback, *The International Film Industry: Western Europe and America Since 1945*, Indiana University Press (Bloomington and London: 1969). A sober, clear-sighted survey of the internationalization of Hollywood's production and distribution activities.

Professor Nicholas Garnham, *The Economics of the US Motion Picture Industry*, XII/206/80/EN, Commission of the European Economic Community (Brussels: 1980). A report appointed by the Commission which offers some bleak conclusions for Community film policy in the face of competition from Hollywood.

Michael Chanan, *Labour Power in the British Film Industry*, British Film Institute (London: 1976). A brief account of the development of trade unionism in the British film industry.

Association of Cinematograph, Television and Allied Technicians, *Action! Fifty Years in the Life of a Trade Union*, ACTT (London: 1983). A lively and popular celebration of the union's history. Well-illustrated.

Edward Buscombe, *Making 'Legend of the Werewolf'*, British Film Institute (London: 1976). A case study of how a feature film is made, here a modest budget horror picture.

John Trevelyan, *What the Censor Saw*, Michael Joseph (London: 1973). A relaxed but informative memoir by the Secretary of the British Board of Film Censors between 1958 and 1971.

Stephen Brody, *Screen Violence and Censorship – A Review of Research, Home Office Research Study No. 40*, HMSO (London: 1977). A rather inflexible review of academic research on the effects of films on viewers. Its final summary questions the naïve assumptions of many politicians and pressure groups.

Report of the Committee on Obscenity and Film Censorship, Cmnd. 7772, HMSO (London: 1979).

Martin Barker (ed.) *The Video Nasties*, Pluto Press (London: 1984). A series of essays looking at the implications for civil liberties of the Video Recordings Act.

The Monopolies Commission, *Films, A Report on the Supply of Films for Exhibition in Cinemas*, HC 206, HMSO, (London: 1966), and the Monopolies and Mergers Commission, *Films, A Report on the Supply of Films for Exhibition in Cinemas*, Cmnd. 8858, HMSO, (London: 1983). Two investigations which clearly show the monopolistic character of the film trade. Much useful material in both reports.

Some of the debates surrounding cinema are argued through in the Open University Course on Popular Culture (U203). The following Course Units are particularly relevant: Unit 7, *British Cinema in the 1930s*; Unit 21, *James Bond as Popular Hero;* and Unit 31/32, *Conclusion*.

Don Macpherson (ed.) *Traditions of Independence, British Cinema in the Thirties*, British Film Institute (London: 1980). A series of essays on the workers' film movement of the 1930s and the lessons for independent film-makers in the 1980s.

Rod Stoneman and Hilary Thompson (eds), *The New Social Function of Cinema: Catalogue of British Film Institute Productions '78/80*, British Film Institute, (London: 1981). Not merely a catalogue but also a collection of essays on new independent British cinema and its social role.

Film Policy, Cmnd. 9319, HMSO (London: 1984). The UK government's White Paper on future film policy. Little analysis but many assertions.

Index

OTHER BOOKS FROM PLUTO

ON TELEVISION
STUART HOOD

Stuart Hood looks at the way the words and images used by television cameras are chosen, who chooses them, what the organizations are in which the broadcasters work, and how these organizations are linked to the central power of the state.

'The best little book about the medium to be published for some time.' *Time Out*
'Needs to read by anyone who thinks television is worth caring about.' *New Society*
'An adept and rounded critique.' Anthony Smith, Director of the BFI

144 pages
0 86104 702 8   £3.50 paperback

THE VIDEO NASTIES
Freedom and Censorship in the Media
Edited by Martin Barker

The parliamentary attack on 'video nasties' was widely acclaimed; liberal opinion was virtually silenced by what was successfully presented as an unprecedented barrage of filthy corrupting material.

Never before in this century has parliament been willing to accept, indeed welcome, so much state censorship. This book presents a reasoned argument about the issues at stake.

Contributors include Martin Barker, Nigel Andrews, Graham Murdock, Geoffrey Pearson, Marco Starr and Brian Brown.

'Valuable and thought-provoking' *Times Educational Supplement*
'One of the most important books' *Sounds*

144 pages
0 86104 667 6   £3.50 paperback

ART/POLITICS/CINEMA
The *Cineaste* Interviews
Edited by Dan Georgakas and Lenny Rubenstein

Thirty-six interviews with Costa-Gavras,
Bertolucci, Sembene, Pontecorvo, Fonda, Rosi,
Wertmuller, Fassbinder, Berger, Wajda,
Zanussi, Ray and other film makers, script
writers and critics.

The interviews cover in depth the major
questions that committed film making must face
up to: its treatment of the Third World, of
feminism and of the cinema, the interplay of the
personal and the political, the gap between
objective truth and cinematic truth – questions
of concern to all film buffs. The interviews first
appeared in *Cineaste*, the leading US radical
film publication.

'The result is a stimulating and provocative
series of interviews... ' *Variety*
'It is this balance between the psychological
and the political on the levels of both life and
art that keeps *Cineaste* interviews on the
cutting edge of film criticism.' *Film Quarterly*

400 pages
0 7453 0014 6   £7.50 paperback

KINO-EYE
The Writings of Dziga Vertov
Edited and introduced by Annette Michelson

In post-revolutionary Russia, Vertov was a prolific film maker – *The Man with the Movie Camera* is now a classic. *Kino-Eye* brings together his agitational writing, extracts from his notebooks and proposals for creative projects. Spanning a period of 30 years (1922-52) *Kino-Eye* portrays Vertov's trajectory from film maker of the revolution to 'non-artist' in the dark years of Stalinism. His writings reflect the commitment of a generation of artists to revolutionary change in form and content. Their first appearance in English is a major contribution to film studies.

344 pages. Illustrated throughout
0 86104 767 2   £19.95 hardback

SIGNED, SEALED AND DELIVERED
True Life Stories of Women in Pop
SUE STEWARD and SHERYL GARRATT

A book about women in the music industry: TV performers and chart inhabitants; label and group managers; women who promote and sell the product, and who damn and praise it in the pages of the music press; and the women on the factory floors of the pressing and packing plants.

Signed, Sealed and Delivered wrily tells it like it is, and discovers the hidden women of music-making.

'A fine overview of how women see themselves in pop.' *New Statesman*

168 pages. Illustrated throughout
0 86104 657 9   £5.95 paperback

POP GOES THE CULTURE
CRAIG McGREGOR
Introduction by Simon Frith

Pop Goes the Culture ranges over jazz, rock
music, Australia, suburban living and equality.
Its central theme is the creation of popular
culture.

The essays in *Pop Goes the Culture* violate
the polite norms of 'high' culture. A 'new
journalist', Craig McGregor brings a radical
populist commitment to his subjects – the jazz of
Harlem and New Orleans, the 'Awfulville'
suburbs of Australia's cities, the humour of
Barry Humphries. His engagement is a
refreshing antidote to the refined detachment of
our cultural establishment.

160 pages
0 86104 750 8   £3.95 paperback

SEEING IS BELIEVING
PETER BISKIND

Hollywood embroiders its dreams and fantasies
out of the themes of the times. In the 1950s the
themes were consensus and dissent, conformity
and individualism, sex and gender,
delinquency, the Commie invasion.

Analysing in detail such classics as *From
Here to Eternity, It Came from Outer Space, On
the Waterfront, Rebel Without a Cause, The
Fountainhead*, Peter Biskind shows how the
industry handled the major 'us and them'
conflicts and the 'us and us' conflicts – between
liberal and conservative capitalists, between
men and women, between organization men
and rugged individualists.

'A fascinating look below the surface of the
movies of the 1950s: *Seeing is Believing* will
make you look at them with different eyes.'
Robert Wise, producer of *West Side Story* and
The Sound of Music

384 pages
0 86104 743 5   £6.95 paperback

THE EMPIRE'S OLD CLOTHES
What the Lone Ranger, Babar and other innocent heroes do to our minds
ARIEL DORFMAN

Ariel Dorfman looks behind some of the best-known characters of popular literature and comics, to the dilemmas they solve, the values they promote.

Along the way, with wit and a wily style, he raises some provocative and disturbing questions. Why do Disney comics teem with uncles and nephews but no mothers and fathers? How could a comic book help to overthrow a government? How does an 'adult's' magazine like *Reader's Digest* continually turn us back into children?

The Empire's Old Clothes is a lucid, entertaining analysis of the connections between politics and culture by a co-author of the widely-read *How to Read Donald Duck*.

Ariel Dorfman was a professor of journalism and literature in Allende's Chile, exiled after September 1973. He is also the author of the powerful novel *Widows*.

240 pages
0 86104 722 2   £4.95 paperback

THEATRE OF THE OPPRESSED
AUGUSTO BOAL

Theatre is being removed from the dead grasp of the ruling class.

Just as Freire showed how language could be a tool for liberation, so Boal restores theatre to its proper place as a popular form of communication and expression. He describes the ways in which theatre came to reflect ruling-class control, and explains how that process can be reversed. The author relates his theory to actual examples in revolutionary theatre in Latin America and to the theatre exercises and games used in the *barrios*.

This book has been described as 'the most important work in the theatre in modern times' and concerns theatre as a rehearsal for revolution.

'Should be read by everyone in the world of theatre who has any pretensions at all to political commitment.' John Arden

224 pages
0 86104 080 5   £4.95 paperback

BEATS OF THE HEART
Popular Music of the World
JEREMY MARRE and HANNAH
CHARLTON

The Saturday night hop, carnival, highdays and
holidays – popular music is associated with all
these occasions. *Beats of the Heart* expands that
image: it looks at the relevance of music for
people keeping their own culture alive in a
changing world, at all levels: newsmaking,
politics, myth and history, as well as celebration
and fantasy. Chinese workers pick rice to
muzak from their local radio station; a Tex Mex
producer distributes his records, hot off the
press, the length of the troubled border; village
kids practise kick boxing to pop music in
Thailand; black workers applaud an all-night
song contest in a Durban hostel. This music is
neither imposed high culture nor subsidized
folklore; it is the music of people experiencing
change and is itself music in transition.

    Beats of the Heart draws on extensive
material gathered in the course of making 14
films in different countries.

    A writer on music and related subjects,
Hannah Charlton is currently an editor on the
Sunday Times magazine. Jeremy Marre is a
documentary film maker of international fame.
His films include the 14-part *Heart Beats* series,
the South Bank Show on Karajan, *Black Music in
Britain* and *The Way of the Sword*, a film on the
martial arts of Japan. He is, at present, filming a
series for Channel Four TV on British popular
music.

256 pages
Illustrated throughout
0 7453 0052 9   £6.95 paperback

THE GREAT MUSEUM
The Re-Presentation of History
DONALD HORNE

As tourism grows, attendances at museums soar. Museums respond to our need to rediscover a past. They fulfil this need by giving us a history: a history that reflects the priorities of those who keep and own the museums.

The Great Museum is a look at European history as reflected in its museums. The book takes up the great subjects – the church, the nation, the rise of capitalism, the labour movement, fascism – and shows how through its museums, each state presents its own view of the past.

The museums visited by Donald Horne include those of Eastern Europe and the Soviet Union; here the intervention of the state in the 'rewriting' of history is very visible.

The book ends by describing the way fascism is presented. It argues that fascism is to be understood as a logical and normal extension of Europe's imperial adventure, and that it is not surprising to find that concentration camps like Dachau are listed in tourist guides under the heading 'Museums and Galleries'! Museums will never be the same again.

Donald Horne is one of Australia's best-known social critics. His book *The Lucky Country* has sold more than a quarter of a million copies.

'This is one of the very few important books, profound books, stimulating books, about museums to have been written during the present century. Coffee-table books and guide-books we have had by the ton, but thinking art books not even by the handful.' *Art Monthly*

272 pages
0 86104 788 5   £5.50 paperback

THE MEDIA MACHINE
JOHN DOWNING

In *The Media Machine* John Downing attempts
to demystify the stabilizing power of the
capitalist media, to encourage the socialist
movement to consider the potentialities of its
own media and at the same time, to provide a
straightforward Marxist account of the media's
handling of three key areas: industrial conflict,
racism and sexism.

'Recommended... succinct... highly
readable'. *Tribune*

230 pages
0 86104 318 9   £4.95 paperback

Pluto books are available through your local
bookshop. In case of difficulty contact Pluto to
find out local stockists or to obtain catalogues/
leaflets (telephone 01-482 1973).
    If all else fails write to:

Pluto Press Limited
Freepost (no stamp required)
105A Torriano Avenue
London NW5 1YP